city baby

city baby

A RESOURCE
FOR NEW YORK PARENTS
FROM PREGNANCY TO PRESCHOOL

KELLY ASHTON AND **PAMELA WEINBERG**

CITY & COMPANY · NEW YORK

Cover illustration copyright © 1997 by Liselotte Watkins
Book design: Leah Lococo   Design assistant: Elizabeth Benator
Back cover photo copyright © 1997 by Manger-Weil Photography

Printed in the United States of America.

Library of Congress Cataloging-in-Publication Data
Weinberg, Pamela.
City baby ; a resource guide for New York parents from pregnancy
to preschool / Pamela Weinberg & Kelly Ashton.
p. cm.
ISBN 1-885492-33-2 (pb)
1. Parents—New York (State)—New York—Handbooks, manuals, etc. 2. Child rearing—New York (State)
—New York—Handbooks, manuals, etc. 3. Children—Services for—New York (State)—New York
—Directories. I. Ashton, Kelly. II. Title.
HQ755.8.W4 1997
649' . 1'09747—dc21   97-2828
CIP

PUBLISHER'S NOTE

Neither City & Company nor the authors have any interest, financial or personal,
in the locations listed in this book. No fees were paid or services rendered in exchange for inclusion
in these pages. Please also note that while every effort was made to ensure that information
regarding phone numbers, hours, admission fees, and prices was accurate at the time of publication,
it is always best to call ahead and verify. Furthermore, readers should discuss all health-related
issues with their medical practitioner before acting.

City & Company books are available at special discounts for premiums and sales promotions.
Special editions can also be created to specification. For details, contact the Sales Director.

City & Company
22 West 23rd Street
New York, NY 10010

**for our city babies:
Alessandro, Rebecca, and Benjamin**

acknowledgments

We would like to thank the following people for their encouragement and support in the writing of this book: Carlo Sant Albano and Matthew Weinberg, Susan and Joel Kastin, Sander and Mechele Flaum, Harris and Angela Ashton, Victoria Ashton, Dave Kahng, Ronni Soled, Anabeth Karson, Howard Applebaum, Christine Wansleban, Christine Keely, Carol Davenport, Gregory Candido, Beth Teitelman, Kiki Schaffer, Waveney Kadir, Lori Robinson, Leah Lococo, Kim Hertlein, Liselotte Watkins, Liza Martin, Sia Sotarakis, Nicole Clifford, Jill Dietz, Janet Siroto, Madeline and Don Wein, Herman Cziment, Rachel Simon, Cassandra Black, Emerson Bruns, Manger-Weil Photography, Kathy Goldman, Jennifer Adams, Stephanie Iverson, Wendy Hubbert, Megan Buckley, and Rifat Salam.

With special thanks and gratitude to Helene Silver of City & Company and Andrea Thompson, our editor, whose invaluable help and advice made this book possible.

contents

introduction

By the time you're ready to be a City Mom, you've probably negotiated a few promotions and raises for yourself, hired and fired a contractor for your home, planned your wedding, and mastered the Internet. So why does having a City Baby seem like such a daunting challenge?

Maybe it's because in a city full of competent women, here's one neighborhood you don't know yet. Fear not. Those competent moms were once in your shoes. Only recently, it was daunting to them too! Now, they've mastered it, though, and they navigate those strollers like champions.

Follow us through the land of City Baby. This book is the creation of two devoted City Moms. We became first-time mothers within a few months of each other, and we swapped pregnancy, childbirth, newborn, and baby stories. As we searched the city for terrific maternity clothes (like a formal dress for the eighth month), adorable baby furniture, exercise classes to keep us fit, and trustworthy child-care help, we realized how much time, energy, and expertise it takes to prepare for a City Baby and settle in as City Parents.

It would have been much easier if somebody had written a book — a central resource — to help us find everything this city offers. So that's why we wrote *City Baby*. We hope it will be that central resource for you, to guide you through the mountains of choices that can paralyze even the smartest New York woman.

We all agree that there is no better place to have a baby than New York City. You'll find everything you will ever need for you and your new son or daughter — and you'll have so many choices of where to find it, do it, and see it. We've done your homework for you: so you'll learn where to take a Lamaze class, how to hire a baby nurse, sign up for baby swim or parenting classes, which restaurants are kid-friendly, which parks and playgrounds are great on a hot summer day, where to throw a great birthday party, and how to choose an indestructible stroller.

We toured hospitals, received pregnancy massages, visited indoor play spaces, shopped every maternity, children's furniture and clothing store, and even checked out rest rooms for mothers and babies. (You won't believe how important this will be to you!)

Throughout the book, we've put asterisks next to our favorite selections to indicate those which we view as the best in each category. We usually provide an address, phone number, and a ballpark price for every item or service but to make your life easier, please call ahead and confirm. Prices, hours, and services are constantly changing.

Keep *City Baby* by the kitchen phone. Take it shopping, You'll use it over and over again. This book contains everything New York has to offer you and your baby. But remember, you can always borrow, trade, make-do, or re-use. It's expensive to live in this great city, and if you can save here and there, all the better. Height-of-fashion clothes or a state-of-the-art crib is not what makes a happy, well-adjusted baby. You — the loving parent — are the most important thing.

You're embarking on an adventure that will take the rest of your life to complete. We hope that *City Baby* will help make your first few years of parenthood easier.

Congratulations! Have a wonderful time, and let us hear from you. If you find a great class or nutritionist or baby resource you think should be included in the next edition of this book, write to us at City & Company, 22 West 23rd Street, New York, NY 10010.

PART ONE

preparing for a city baby:

everything you need to know

1 · from obstetric care to childbirth

Congratulations! The pregnancy test is positive, and in nine months, you'll give birth to a beautiful baby. Tell the prospective grandparents, aunts, and uncles of the new addition to the clan, then start making the decisions that will keep you busy for the next nine months. First, you will have to consider:

> *Who will provide you with prenatal care throughout your pregnancy?*
> *Who will deliver your baby?*
> *Where will your baby be born?*

Who will look after you and your baby during your pregnancy? Basically, you have two choices: a doctor (who may be the obstetrician/gynecologist you saw in your pre-pregnancy days or another doctor you select at this time) or a midwife. Both of these professionals will perform essentially the same service—meet with you during your pregnancy to monitor your progression and help deliver your baby on the big day.

Where your baby will be born is easy: a hospital, a birthing center, or at home. Yes, the occasional New York City baby has been known to make her entrance in a taxi cab in the middle of the Triborough Bridge, but it's a remote possibility. You'll probably make it to the right place on time.

You have had the good sense (or blind luck) to be having a baby in a city that seems to have an obstetrician on every other block and some of the best hospitals in the world. Finding excellent care won't be a problem.

This chapter provides everything you need to know about the birthing business in New York—doctors, midwives, hospitals, birthing centers, childbirth preparation classes, labor coaches, lactation consultants, and more.

THE BIRTH ATTENDANT

Whether it's an obstetrician or midwife, you will want to choose this person as soon as you discover you're pregnant.

Obstetricians

Most women in New York deliver their babies in a hospital under the care of an obstetrician. You probably already have an obstetrician/gynecologist whom you've been seeing for annual checkups, and you may be perfectly happy to continue on together throughout your pregnancy. But you may want to find a new doctor for one of several reasons: your current ob/gyn is fine for the routine checkups, but friends have told you about a wonderful new doctor; your ob/gyn is farther away from your apartment than you'd like; your ob/gyn is affiliated with a hospital that doesn't appeal to you; or you may be over thirty-five years old, considered high risk, and want an ob/gyn who specializes in high-risk pregnancies.

If you're comfortable and happy with your current ob/gyn, stick with her. If you would like to find someone else, do so. With the large number of good obstetricians in New York, you can afford to pick and choose. To find an obstetrician:

Ask friends who have had babies or the mother down the hall in your apartment building. A recommendation based on the personal experience of a woman who's already been through what you're just beginning is a good way to go.

❋ Ask your internist or general practitioner to recommend an obstetrician.

❋ Call the hospital where you would like to deliver, and ask for a referral from their obstetrical department. (After you check out the hospital chart starting on page 27, you may find a hospital that is especially suited to your needs.)

✳ Go to the library and look up *New York Magazine*'s most recent "The Best Doctors in New York" issue.

✳ Call the New York County Medical Society (399-9040) for a listing of obstetricians who practice in the city.

Once you have a candidate or two, call for a consultation. Any doctor should be willing to sit down with you and discuss what you can expect over the next nine months and during the birth. Come for your appointment armed with a list of questions, a pen and pad, and your husband or partner—two listeners are better than one.

After this initial consultation, you should be able to decide whether this is the doctor for you. He or she should listen to you carefully, answer your questions thoroughly, and inspire your trust. You need to feel confident that this doctor will be there for you any time night or day during your pregnancy. Here are some questions that you should ask:

Are you part of a group practice? If so, will I see the other doctors in the practice? What is the likelihood that you will deliver my baby, rather than one of your colleagues?

✳ How often will I need to have an office visit?

✳ What tests should I expect to have and when?

✳ What is the fee for a vaginal birth? Cesarean birth? What extra charges should I expect? (Note: many good doctors now charge the same fee for a vaginal or cesarean delivery, because they do not want to be accused of performing unnecessary cesareans.)

✳ What are your thoughts on natural childbirth, anesthesia, episiotomy, cesarean section, induction of labor? (Ask these and any other questions about the doctor's birthing philosophy that are of concern to you.)

✳ With which hospital are you affiliated? Does the hospital have birthing rooms; labor, delivery, and recovery rooms; rooming-in for baby and husband; a neonatal intensive care unit?

✳ What do you consider "high risk" birth factors?

✳ How do I get answers to my questions between visits? If you are busy, is there another doctor in the office who will take my call?

✳ Do you have nurses trained to answer basic prenatal questions? (Obstetricians spend half their day doing hospital deliveries or patient check-ins, so it is important to know that if your doctor is not there, someone will be available to answer your questions in a timely manner.)

While you're at the doctor's office for your consultation, check out the waiting room. If you can, ask one or two of the pregnant women, who'll probably be leafing through the latest *Parents* magazine, how long they usually wait to see the doctor. Routine visits should take about ten minutes, and there is nothing more frustrating than waiting one hour for a ten-minute visit. Also, ask whether the doctor works in a collaborative way with patients, making joint decisions, or whether he likes to call the shots.

The usual schedule for visiting your ob/gyn in a low-risk, normal pregnancy is every three weeks for the first seven months, every two weeks in the eighth month, and every week in the ninth month. Of course, this may vary with different practices, and if your pregnancy is high risk you may see your doctor more often.

Some common tests to expect in the course of your pregnancy are:

Sonogram. Typically a woman has two or three sonograms (ultrasounds) during her pregnancy. The first will be done in the second month (about nine weeks) to date her pregnancy; the second will be done in the fifth month (about twenty weeks) to check the growth and internal organs of the fetus; and a third may be done in the ninth month (about thirty-six weeks) to get an idea of the baby's size and position.

✳ *MSAFP* (Maternal Serum Alpha-Fetoprotein Screening). The MSAFP screening is performed in the fourth month (sixteen to eighteen weeks). This simple blood test determines the levels of alpha-fetoprotein (blood protein) present in the mother's blood. A high or low level *may* indicate some serious problems in the development of the fetus. However, if the MSAFP level comes back either too high or too low, the doctor will probably recommend a second test to check the results.

✳ *Amniocentesis.* Known to moms as an amnio, this procedure is performed in the fourth month (sixteen to eighteen weeks) of pregnancy. The technician, guided by an ultrasound image of the uterus, inserts a long hollow needle through the woman's abdominal wall and withdraws a small amount of amniotic fluid. Amniocentesis is recommended for women over thirty-five (although many women over thirty choose to have it performed as well) and in cases in which genetic disorders or chromosomal abnormalities might be suspected.

Most of these tests and procedures are routine, and the obstetrician you choose will have conducted, ordered, or overseen them on hundreds of pregnant women before you. But your pregnancy is unique to you, and you should feel perfectly comfortable asking what you may consider dumb questions about the need for tests and the meaning of their results. Always ask.

If you are thirty-five or older, you may be considered high risk. Statistics show that women over thirty-five have a slightly greater risk of problems during pregnancy. Other circumstances can also determine a high-risk pregnancy—a previous period of infertility, multiple miscarriages, high blood pressure, diabetes, obesity, or other serious health problems. Make sure your doctor takes your full medical history.

A number of obstetricians specialize in high-risk pregnancies. *New York Magazine*'s "The Best Doctors in New York" issue lists many of them. Your own ob/gyn can also refer you to such a specialist. Or call the obstetrical department of any of the hospitals (listed on page 27), and ask for a referral based upon your specific needs.

Midwives

A fair number of New York women opt for a midwife, rather than an obstetrician, to lead them through their pregnancy and delivery. A midwife may be a good fit for you if you're low risk, and if you like the idea of working one-on-one with someone. A midwife will most likely be more available than an obstetrician to talk with you about the emotional aspects of what you're experiencing, and will probably be more oriented toward natural childbirth.

If this sounds good to you, you will want to find a Certified Nurse Midwife (CNM), a registered nurse who has undergone extensive formal training through an accredited nurse-midwifery program. The American College of Nurse Midwives, based in Washington, D.C., provides midwife certification nationally and sets the standards for the practice of nurse-midwifery. Only ACNM–certified midwives are able to practice in hospitals.

Two other categories of midwives are Direct Entry Midwives, often referred to as Lay Midwives, and Physician-Assistant Midwives.

The latter may also be certified through the ACNM and therefore can practice in hospitals. Direct Entry Midwives, trained through a combination of coursework and apprenticeship, are not permitted to practice in hospitals but do perform or assist at many home births in the New York City area.

When you choose a CNM, find out about her hospital affiliation. You may prefer to deliver in a birthing center or at home, but in the event of a medical complication, it is critical that your practitioner has access to a hospital nearby. Many CNMs in New York do practice in hospitals and will deliver your baby in the same birthing rooms that the obstetricians use.

With a CNM, you can expect the same type of schedule you would have with an obstetrician: a visit every three or four weeks at the beginning of your pregnancy; every three weeks in the seventh month; every two weeks in the eighth month; and every week in the ninth month. Like an obstetrician, the midwife will ask how you are feeling and if you have any questions. She will give you an external exam, take your blood pressure and weight, and listen to the baby's heartbeat.

If you would like to check out midwifery, call any of the names listed here, and set up an appointment for a consultation, just as you would for an obstetrician. Use the list of questions we have provided for choosing an obstetrician (see page 19). In addition, you may be especially interested in learning how the midwife plans to help you through the stages of labor and delivery, the point at which the practices of CNMs and obstetricians usually differ. Many CNMs are skilled at relaxing and preparing the perineum so that anesthesia and episiotomies are rarely necessary. CNMs cannot administer epidurals or other prescription pain medications.

The following is a list of the hospital-based independent practices of Certified Nurse Midwives in New York City:

Silvie Blaustein/Shawn Reitman
(affiliated with Beth Israel South)
CNM/OB Practice 545-9300
461 Park Avenue South at 31st Street

Beth Israel Midwifery Group
Beth Israel Medical Center 844-8569
Phillips Ambulatory Care Center
10 Union Square East

CBS Midwifery, Inc.

Barbara Sellars/Cynthia Casoff

(affiliated with St. Vincent's)

103 Fifth Avenue at 17th Street 366-4699

Midwifery Services, Inc.

(affiliated with St. Luke's-Roosevelt)

135 West 70th Street 877-5556

Maureen Rayson Associates, Inc.

(affiliated with St. Vincent's)

420 West 23rd Street 989-9510

Note: You and your doctor or midwife should decide jointly, based on your wishes and her expertise, on a birthing plan for the big day. Sometime after you begin your visits, but well before your due date, decide what will happen regarding anesthesia, IVs, and episiotomies. Your ideal birthing plan (barring any unexpected surprises) should be in writing, in your doctor's file, and on hand at the hospital when you arrive.

THE BIRTH PLACE
Hospitals

All obstetricians are affiliated with a hospital, or maybe two, so once you have selected your obstetrician, you will deliver at her hospital.

If you are still in the process of choosing an obstetrician, you may want to work backward—find the hospital you prefer, and then find an agreeable obstetrician who practices there. Knowing as much as you can about the place your baby will be born is very helpful and comforting.

Here's what's important to know about the hospital: the number of birthing rooms, cesarean rate, level of care provided in the neonatal unit, policies on husbands in the delivery room, rooming-in (husband and baby staying overnight in your room), and sibling and family visitors. New York has many hospitals, but some are newer and more comfortable than others. Mount Sinai and Roosevelt hospitals have decorated their labor, delivery, and recovery rooms with Laura Ashley–like touches, so they feel more like a bedroom than a hospital room. While it may be tempting to choose a hospital based upon decor, trust us when we tell you that once you are in labor, the color of the wallpaper in the labor room will be the last thing on your mind. New York Hospital is one of the oldest (they recently renovated, and a new wing opened earlier this year): it has an excellent reputation. However, when Kelly delivered there, her

Top Ten Hospital Tips

1. Decide whether you want a private room *before* you go into labor.
2. Bring a pillow with a colored pillowcase from home.
3. Bring your robe and slippers.
4. Bring a bath towel and washcloth. (Hospital towels are tiny!)
5. Bring sanitary napkins.
6. Have a friend or family member present as much as possible to go for drinks, run errands, and get the nurse.
7. Have key phone numbers with you—baby nurse, furniture delivery, mohel, etc.
8. Call your insurance company as soon as possible after the baby is born.
9. Rest as much as possible: you are not going to get much rest for the next ten years.
10. Let the nurse feed the baby at 2 or 3 A.M. if you are not exclusively breast feeding. You need your sleep!

changed since she delivered Kelly!

We toured all the private hospitals in New York City where babies are delivered and found them to be similar in many ways. They provide birthing beds, showers, or squatting bars to help your labor and delivery. And in most, if not all, cases, it is your own doctor or mid-wife—not the hospital or staff—who makes the important decisions concerning your labor.

Other general points to keep in mind:

All the hospitals allow you to preregister. This is a good idea, because once you are in labor, you won't want to fill out forms—registering in advance can keep the paperwork to a minimum upon your arrival.

✳ Check your insurance company's policy on length of hospital stay permitted for child-birth. Most insurance companies cover either a twenty-four or forty-eight-hour stay for a vaginal delivery and three to four days for a cesarean delivery.

✳ Contact your insurance company when you become pregnant so that later there won't be any problems with the forms you submit. Some insurance companies require notification before you check into the hospital.

✳ Private rooms are available at each of these hospitals. But keep in mind that the cost of a

mother commented that it was easy to find her because the maternity floor hadn't private room is not covered by insurance—your out-of-pocket expenses will range from $100 to $250 per night. Rooming-in for husbands and newborns is permitted in all hospitals in a private room. (In some hospitals it is also permitted in a semiprivate room as long as your roommate doesn't object.)

✳ All the hospitals have twenty-four-hour parking lots nearby (they will provide you with a list). Find out which hospital entrance to use in case you arrive in the middle of the night.

✳ All hospitals offer weekly classes for new mothers—bathing the baby, breastfeeding, and basic child care. If you cannot make it to a class, ask the nurses, who are trained to help. From our own experience, you must ask to have these lessons. You are in charge, so speak up about your needs.

✳ Many of the hospitals have extremely generous visiting hours. The nurse conducting our tour at New York Hospital gave excellent advice in this regard: She said to be selfish and careful about your visitors for your own health and well-being and for that of the baby. Use your hospital stay to get some rest, if possible, and to bond with your baby. There will be plenty of time for visitors when you and your baby get home.

✳ Bring two pillows from home for your postpartum room. You will be a lot more comfortable sleeping on your own pillows, as most hospital pillows are flat as a board. Make sure your pillow cases are any color but white so they don't get mixed in with the hospital laundry.

After touring ten hospitals, we became experts at predicting the questions we'd most often hear from fellow expectant parents:

Can we bring music into the delivery room?

✳ Can the baby be wrapped in a receiving blanket that we bring from home instead of a regulation hospital blanket?

✳ Can we dim the lights in the labor room?

✳ Can my husband/partner cut the umbilical cord?

The answer to all these questions is yes, but we can tell you that once labor begins your only concern is delivering that baby any way you can, music or no music.

The following chart provides information to consider while evaluating the hospital in which you will deliver your baby. It includes:

Hospital: The name, address, key phone numbers and visiting hours.

Labor rooms: The number and type of delivery rooms. In a labor, delivery, and recovery room, known as an LDR room, you will do just that before you are transferred to a post-partum room. If the hospital has a labor, delivery, recovery, and post-partum room, LDRP, you will remain there your entire hospital stay, but few hospitals have them. An operating room is where cesareans and complicated vaginal births take place. A labor room is for labor only. A delivery room is where you will be taken when you are ten centimeters dilated and ready to deliver. From delivery you go to a recovery room for one to two hours before going to your own room where you will stay until you leave the hospital.

Midwives: Hospitals with midwives on staff, and those which allow midwives to deliver babies.

Cesarean birthrate: Numbers indicate the percentage of births by cesarean section each year. The percentages listed are from 1991 (the most recent published figures) unless otherwise indicated. Generally, hospitals with midwives have the lowest rates; hospitals with a large infertility/high-risk patient base have the highest.

Nursery level: Neonatal intensive care units are classified in Levels I through IV, with Level IV being the most advanced. Choosing a hospital with a Level III or Level IV nursery is recommended, especially for high-risk pregnancies.

Childbirth classes: Prenatal classes for women and their husbands or partners, including Lamaze, breastfeeding, and preparation for cesarean birth. These classes are given at the hospital (unless otherwise noted), and you must sign up in advance.

Other information: Any unique features about the hospital.

HOSPITAL	LABOR RMS/OTHER	CLASSES
Beth Israel Hospital 16th St. & 1st Ave. 420-2000 (General) 420-2999 (Classes) 420-2935 (Patient Care) VISITING HOURS: 11 A.M.–8 P.M. (flexible for father)	12 LDR (6 recently renovated with showers) MIDWIVES: Yes CESAREAN RATE: 17.9% NURSERY LEVEL III Has mother/baby nursing (family centered—the same nurse takes care of you and your baby).	Lamaze; Early Pregnancy; Baby Care Basics; Breast-feeding; Preparation for Childbirth; Sibling Preparation; Preparation for Parenthood; New Mother Support Group; CPR; Child Safety
Columbia Presbyterian Hospital/Babies Hospital/ Sloane Hospital for Women Broadway & 166th St. 305-2500 (General) 305-2040 (Parent Ed.) VISITING HOURS: General: 6:30–8 P.M. Fathers: 8 A.M.–10 P.M. Grandparents: 12–8 P.M. Siblings: 3:30–4:30 P.M.	7 LDR/3 Delivery MIDWIVES: No CESAREAN RATE: 20–22% (1995) NURSERY LEVEL III Aesthetically the most impressive. Spacious post-partum rooms are beautifully decorated, with bathroom and shower. Moms bring baby to post-partum floor by themselves—provides nice bonding time. On-staff post-natal masseuse available.	Preparation for Childbirth; Breastfeeding; Cesarean Birth; Sibling Tours
Lenox Hill Hospital 100 E. 77th St. 434-2000 (General) 434-2238 (Parent Ed.) 434-3152 (Babies' Club)	6 Labor/2 Birthing and LDR 4 Delivery/1 Recovery MIDWIVES: No CESAREAN RATE: 32.9% NURSERY LEVEL III LDR in one room.	Preparation for Cesarean; "Now That You're Pregnant" Seminar; CPR; Infant Care; Infant Massage; Breastfeeding; Childbirth Refresher;

HOSPITAL	LABOR RMS/OTHER	CLASSES

Lenox Hill continued
VISITING HOURS:
  Father: Anytime
  Family: 3–8 P.M.
  General: 12–1:30 P.M.;
    7–8 P.M.
	Request birthing room for best experience.	Sibling Preparation

The Mount Sinai Medical Center
One Gustave L. Levy Place
Klingenstein Pavilion
5th Ave. at 98th St.
241-6500 (General)
241-7491 (Women's
  & Children's Office)
241-6578 (Breastfeeding
  Warm Line)
VISITING HOURS:
  Father: 10 A.M.–10 P.M.
  General: 12–1:30 P.M.;
    7–8 P.M.
	13 LDR/1 Recovery (holds 5 women)
	3 Operating Rooms
	MIDWIVES: No. Midwives cannot deliver babies at Mt. Sinai, but with permission of OB/GYN, they can be in the Labor Room.
	CESAREAN RATE: 18.7%
	NURSERY LEVEL IV
	LDR rooms decorated in country motif—resemble hotel rooms more than hospital rooms.
		Novice Lamaze; Caring for Newborns; Breastfeeding; Sibling Preparation for Children 2 1/2–7 yrs.; Preparation for Cesarean: Classes held at 5 E. 98th St.

NY Hospital/Cornell Medical Center 525 E. 68th St. 746-5454 (General) 746-3215 (Parenthood Prep.)	8 Labor/3 Birthing and LDR 3 Delivery/1 Recovery MIDWIVES: No CESAREAN RATE: 25–30% (1995)	Lamaze; Breastfeeding; Baby Care; Adapting to Parenthood; New Mother Support Group

HOSPITAL	LABOR RMS/OTHER	CLASSES
NY Hospital/Cornell **continued** VISITING HOURS: Father: Anytime General: 11 A.M.–8 P.M.	NURSERY LEVEL IV Semi-private rooms sleep four.	
New York University **Medical Center** 560 1st Ave. (32nd St.) 263-7300 (General) 263-7201 (Classes) VISITING HOURS: Father, Family: 8:30 A.M.–8:30 P.M. General: 1:30–8:30 P.M.	2 Birthing (LDR)/5 Labor 1 Recovery/3 Delivery MIDWIVES: No CESAREAN RATE: 34% NURSERY LEVEL IV Spacious Birthing Rooms (LDR) with rockers, wood floors. Request upon arrival in Labor.	Prepared Childbirth; Prepared Childbirth Review; Accelerated Childbirth; Cesarean Birth; Sibling Class; Breast-feeding; Breastfeeding Support Group
Roosevelt Hospital 1000 Tenth Ave. (59th St.) 523-4000 (General) 523-6222 (Classes) VISITING HOURS: Father: 10 A.M.–10 P.M. (24 hrs. for private room) Sibling: 11 A.M.–8 P.M.	7 LDR/4 LDRP MIDWIVES: Yes. Midwives deliver in LDR rooms at Birthing Center. CESAREAN RATE: 22.3% NURSERY LEVEL III New and attractive facilities. Only NYC birth center attached to hospital. Center has jacuzzis, kitchen, allows siblings to observe birth.	Lamaze; Refresher Childbirth Course; Vaginal Birth After Cesarean; Baby Care; Infant CPR; You and the Baby CPR; Child CPR; Sibling Preparation Class

HOSPITAL	LABOR RMS/OTHER	CLASSES
St. Luke's Hospital 1111 Amsterdam Ave. (114th St.) 523-4000 (General) 523-6222 (Parent/ Family Ed.) VISITING HOURS: Father: 8:00 A.M.–10 P.M. General: 6:30–8:00 P.M.	5 LDR/2 OR/1 Recovery MIDWIVES: Yes CESAREAN RATE: less than 20% NURSERY LEVEL III Huge private rooms—two-bed rooms used for one woman if requested. Least expensive private room at $100 extra per night. Rooms have own showers.	All classes given at Roosevelt hospital location.
St. Vincent's Hospital & Medical Center 153 W. 11th St. (7th Ave.) 604-7000 (General) 604-7946 (Maternity Ed.) VISITING HOURS: Father, Siblings, Grandparents: 10 A.M.–10 P.M. General: 3–4:30 P.M.; 7–8:30 P.M.	8 LDR/2 OR/1 Recovery MIDWIVES: Yes CESAREAN RATE: 17% (1995) NURSERY LEVEL III Sunny and spacious private rooms with two beds. Family-centered care— mom and baby share same nurse.	Preparation for Childbirth; Childbirth Refresher; Breastfeeding; Newborn Care; Welcome to Parenthood

Birthing Centers

If you choose a midwife, she may deliver at one of the hospitals listed above or at a birthing center. Many women find the non-hospital-like atmosphere and amenities of the birthing center enormously appealing.

Not only your husband or coach, but your mother, father, best friend, and your new baby's older brother or sister can be with you throughout your birth experience. During your labor you can usually walk around, sip tea, or relax in a Jacuzzi or tub—all of which many women find more labor-enhancing and less alarming than being in a hospital bed hooked up to a monitor. At a birthing center, you can choose to labor, and even deliver, your baby in a special tub of soothing warm water!

One caveat to delivering at a birthing center: You must be committed to a natural childbirth. No pain relief, such as Demerol or an epidural block, can be administered.

Two birthing centers exist in Manhattan:

Elizabeth Seton Childbearing Center
(affiliated with St. Vincent's Hospital)
222 West 14th Street 777-5000

The Birthing Center
(attached to St. Luke's-Roosevelt
Hospital Center)
1000 Tenth Avenue at 59th Street
523-BABY

If the idea of a birthing center is appealing, call either of these to schedule a tour and an interview with the director. At both, you can ask for a CNM referral. Or, call a midwife who is affiliated with one of the centers (see pages 22-23) and schedule a consultation.

Note: Ask detailed questions about what procedures the center follows should a medical emergency arise at the time of delivery.

CHILDBIRTH METHODS

Once the *who* and the *where* of your pregnancy and delivery have been settled, you will start to focus—more and more as you grow and grow—on the *how* of it all. What are the best, easiest, most pain–free ways to get that baby out?

As you talk with other pregnant women and new mothers, you will hear about the relative merits of one birthing technique over another. Here is a very short course on the three most well-known and popular.

The Lamaze Method. This method, named after its developer, Dr. Fernand Lamaze, head of an obstetrical clinic in Paris in 1950, is popularly, if not entirely accurately, known as childbirth without pain. The method combines learned breathing techniques (the hoo-hoo-hoo, hee-hee-hee) used during contractions, with relaxation exercises designed to help a woman get through labor comfortably.

Most hospitals listed (see page 27) offer Lamaze classes. Call to sign up. (Also, most of the obstetrical nurses listed are trained in Lamaze and can assist your coach in the labor room if needed.) Couples usually begin Lamaze in the seventh month.

Some large obstetrical practices also offer

Lamaze or will make referrals to private instructors, so ask your obstetrician or midwife. Kelly took Lamaze with Fritzi Kallop (906-9255) and was very happy with her. Kallop, formerly an R.N. at New York Hospital, has published an excellent book on Lamaze called *Fritzi Kallop's Birth Book.* Fritzi is very funny and down to earth, answers questions day and night, and is there for you long after the birth of your little one.

The Bradley Method Husband-Coached Childbirth. This method was developed by Dr. Robert A. Bradley, a Toronto-based obstetrician. The Bradley Method is based on a calming pattern of relaxation, deep abdominal breathing, and close teamwork between husband and wife. Bradley's goal is a completely unmedicated pregnancy (no aspirin or cold remedies) and labor and birth (no epidural block or Pitocin).

With Bradley, the pregnant woman learns various positions for first, second, and third stage labor. She is encouraged to approach her entire pregnancy as training for labor and to prepare her muscles for birth and her breasts for nursing.

Few New York City hospitals offer Bradley instruction for childbirth. To find the name of a certified Bradley instructor in your area, write to The American Academy of Husband-Coached Childbirth, P.O. Box 5224, Sherman Oaks, CA 91413. Or call 800-4-ABIRTH.

Water Labor and Water Birth. Water birth, popular in Russia since the 1960s, has attracted a small but enthusiastic number of supporters in the United States over the last decade or so. Studies have shown that warm water can reduce the hours and stress of labor, offer support to the laboring woman, and help relax blood flow, making the baby's journey into the world easier.

Some women use this method's water-filled tub only as a comfort during labor. Others deliver while still in the tub, and the baby takes his first breaths while most of his body is submerged in water, a gentle and familiar medium from his time in the womb.

The Birthing Center at Roosevelt hospital makes water labor and water birth available as an option. Our friend Judy delivered her daughter there with Judith Halek attending (see below) and was thrilled with her experience. Should you wish, you can rent a birthing tub and have a water birth at home with the help of a midwife.

CHILDBIRTH EDUCATORS, CLASSES, AND OTHER RESOURCES

If you are having a normal pregnancy, you're happy with your OB or CNM, and you've signed up for childbirth education/Lamaze classes through your doctor's office or hospital—congratulations! You are in good shape for a successful pregnancy and delivery.

If you want to know even more about what's going on with your body and what's to come during pregnancy, labor, delivery, and after, New York has many experts who work on a one-on-one basis or in a small group.

Here is a list of resources. These private practitioners specialize in a variety of birth-related areas: Lamaze, Bradley, water birth, labor support, and childbirth education. Some practitioners offer more than one kind of service; make some phone calls, and you may find just the right combination for you.

Fees for childbirth education classes range from $200 to $300 for a four-week session. If you use more than one service from a practitioner, you can probably negotiate a package deal.

The following are specialists in pregnancy and childbirth education:

Felicia Brodzky, AAHCC
2473 Broadway at 92nd Street
496-1889

Felicia is certified in the Bradley Method of childbirth and offers an eight-week course to achieve a drug-free, husband-coached birth. Her classes cover prenatal nutrition, exercise, breastfeeding, birth education, and relaxation techniques. Felicia is studying to become a Certified Nurse Midwife.

Judith Halek
309 West 109th Street
222-4349

Judith is a labor support coach, birthing counselor/educator, and a specialist in pre- and postnatal massage and fitness. She offers private or semiprivate childbirth education classes that cover a variety of topics, including anatomy of pregnancy, diet and nutrition, and water labor and water birth. She attended the first New York City water birth in 1987, runs the East Coast Resource Center for Water Birth, and is a water birth consultant. She also is a birth documentarian and will videotape or photograph labor and birth. Judith works with clients in their home, birth center, or hospital.

Anabeth Karson
309 West 109th Street
222-9227

Anabeth, a shiatsu therapist, holds private prenatal education classes for women and couples and does labor support. She works with clients in their homes or in hers. She is the vice-president of ICAN/NY (International Cesarean Awareness Network).

Cynthia Marsland
244 West 72nd Street
864-6924

Cynthia has been teaching Lamaze for seven years. An experienced labor and delivery nurse and an ASPO certified Lamaze instructor, she teaches private Lamaze and VBAC (Vaginal Birth After Cesarean) classes to women (and their partners) in their homes. She also offers a childbirth refresher class for women who are pregnant for the second time.

Diana Simkin
210 East 86th Street
348-0208

Diana has been offering fitness classes for pre and postnatal women for eighteen years. She gives private or group Lamaze classes, and rents Medela breast pumps. Diana has written three books on pregnancy: *The Complete Pregnancy Exercise Program*, *The Complete Baby Exercise Program*, and *Preparation for Birth*.

Nancy Vega
206 West 104th Street
316-6337

Nancy founded ICAN/NY and is a childbirth educator, a lactation consultant, and home VBAC specialist. She offers private classes for women and couples.

Martine Jean-Baptiste
136 West 81st Street
769-4578

Martine, a registered nurse, has been a labor and delivery nurse for over six years and has been practicing professional labor support and childbirth education for more than two years. She teaches private childbirth education classes for couples in their homes or in her home and will occasionally teach a group class.

Gayatri Martin

220 East 26th Street

725-1078

Gayatri, a registered nurse, teaches child-birth education and prenatal classes and is a certified holistic birth instructor. A holistic birth instructor helps women deal with the psychological and emotional aspects of birth, using body-centered hypnosis. Gayatri creates audio tapes for her clients. She has been a yoga instructor for ten years and also teaches Shiatsu. She is available for private sessions and leads groups sessions in hospitals and in her home.

Mia Borgatta

185 Bowery

529-4720

Mia has been a labor support practitioner and a yoga instructor for seven years and a pre and postnatal massage therapist for ten years. She works independently and will travel to your home or have you come to hers. For women interested in home water birth, she also rents out birthing tubs.

Well-Care Center

161 Madison Avenue at 23rd Street

696-9256

The Well-Care Center is a new group started by Beverly Solo and Laura Best, R.N., formerly lactation consultants at Beth Israel Hospital. The center offers lactation consulting, childbirth education classes with a technique that combines the Lamaze and Bradley methods, labor support, prenatal and post-partum exercise classes, and classes in infant CPR and nutrition. It also trains doulas for the agency In A Family Way.

The International Cesarean Awareness Network (ICAN)/NY Chapter

426 Greenwich Street

974-0973 ext. 700

ICAN is an international grass roots organization that was formed to lower the cesarean rate through education. The group provides a support network for women (and their husbands or partners) who have suffered from trauma after having a cesarean. ICAN also provides a forum for childbirth options, and many midwives, labor coaches, childbirth educators, and water birth experts are members. ICAN/NY is run by Christine Wade.

2 · taking care of yourself

Once you have assembled your support team—from Lamaze instructor to lactation consultant—and checked out the hospital room or birthing center in which your baby will first set eyes on the world, and if you feel comfortable with the choices you have made, it's time to be good to yourself.

Pamela's friend Debby, who didn't appear pregnant until her seventh month, had perfect skin and hair that got thicker and shinier. She looked and acted as if she felt like a million bucks. We consider her the luckiest woman we know. If, as has been true for many of us, the weight gain, bulging belly, and tiredness are making you feel unattractive, now is the time to pamper and indulge yourself. Take advantage of some of the terrific body-strengthening and spirit-lifting services New York has to offer. Treat yourself to a manicure when you're in your ninth month and feel as though you can't stand to be pregnant for one more day.

Most importantly, get involved, early in these nine months, with a physical fitness program that will help you feel your best throughout your pregnancy *and* help you prepare for labor. Our friend Matty worked until ten days before her delivery, taking the subway from her upper West Side apartment to her downtown East Side office and back again every day. She said climbing up and down all those stairs, carrying what turned out to be her ten and one-half pound son, gave her legs of steel. This is good. Strong leg muscles are useful for getting you through the last months of pregnancy, as well as labor and birth.

You can do even more for yourself by checking out one or another of the facilities described in this chapter. You'll find information about health clubs, exercise studios, and private practitioners that offer pre- and post-natal exercise classes, fitness training, yoga, and massage, all fine-tuned and appropriate for pregnant women.

Kelly swears by the Medical Massage Group; the massages she had there relaxed her and the foot reflexology helped her morning sickness. Pamela took prenatal exercise classes twice a week with Lori MaRose (now teaching at World Gym), and had monthly massages with Barbara Close. Most of our pregnant friends have participated in one or another of these programs, and all have been glad they did.

EXERCISE

Most experts agree that exercising throughout your pregnancy is safe, healthy, and beneficial to your overall well-being. If your pregnancy is low risk and normal, you can participate in a moderate exercise program throughout your nine months. If you're a long-time jock or have exercised regularly prior to pregnancy (at least three times per week), you should be able to safely maintain that level of activity, with some modifications, throughout pregnancy and postpartum. Of course, check with your obstetrician or midwife before starting or continuing any exercise regimen, whether you are in the low- or high-risk category. Also be aware of the following recommendations adapted from guidelines issued by the American College of Obstetricians and Gynecologists (ACOG):

Regular exercise (at least three times per week) is preferable to intermittent activity.

❋ **Avoid exercise flat on your back after the fourth month. Lying on your back is associated with decreased cardiac output in pregnancy. Also avoid prolonged periods of standing.**

❋ **During pregnancy, you have less oxygen available for aerobic exercise. Modify the intensity of your exercise according to how you feel. Stop exercising when fatigued, and never exercise to the point of exhaustion.**

Top Ten Tips for Prenatal Exercising

1. Do it!
2. Try as many classes as necessary until you find one you like.
3. Remember to do your Kegels.
4. Don't lie on your back after the fourth month.
5. Drink plenty of water.
6. Don't exercise on an empty stomach; make sure to have a snack first.
7. Exercise with other pregnant women; you won't feel as big.
8. Try yoga for excellent stretching and relaxation.
9. Don't let your heart rate exceed 140 beats per minute.
10. Consult your obstetrician before starting any kind of new exercise.

✳ Weight-bearing exercises such as jogging, may be continued throughout pregnancy, though at lower intensities. Nonweight-bearing exercises, such as cycling and swimming, will minimize the risk of injury.

✳ Avoid exercise that could cause you to lose your balance, especially in the third trimester. Avoid any type of exercise involving the potential for even mild abdominal trauma.

✳ Be sure to eat enough prior to your workout. Pregnancy requires an additional 300 calories per day just to maintain your weight.

✳ Drink water and wear comfortable clothing to augment heat dissipation during exercise.

Many of the body changes of pregnancy persist four to six weeks postpartum. After your baby is born, resume your prepregnancy routines gradually, according to how you feel.

Fitness/Health Clubs

If you don't already have an exercise routine and want to get started, walking is a great and safe way to stay in shape. For those who desire a more structured work-out environment, the following health clubs offer special classes and/or training for pregnant women. Many personal trainers in these health clubs are certified to work with pre- and postnatal women; if you are interested, just inquire. (In many clubs, pregnant women work out right next to their nonpregnant counterparts.)

Membership in most full-service health

clubs (Equinox, New York Sports Club, New York Health & Racquet Club, Vertical Club, and David Barton) ranges from $800 to $1,500 per year, with first-time initiation fees in the $200 to $500 range. These fees are often negotiable and may be discounted based upon corporate affiliations, if you join with a friend or spouse, or if you pay the entire amount upon joining. The fee for a personal trainer varies from club to club, ranging from $50 to more than $100 per hour. With some club memberships, you can use all locations in the chain; others limit work-out locations.

Private clubs offer pleasant accoutrements—roomy changing areas, lots of towels, and nice snack bars. If money is an object, check out the Y classes.

David Barton

30 East 85th Street 517-7577
552 Avenue of the Americas at 15th Street
727-0004

David Barton offers personal trainers who are specialists in working with prenatal women and will design a regimen that is right for your level of fitness. For postpartum women, Barton offers Strollercize classes in which women bring their babies in strollers and perform a series of exercises using the strollers as resistance. These classes are included in the fee for gym membership. There is no baby-sitting available.

Equinox

344 Amsterdam Ave. at 76th Street
721-4200
2465 Broadway at 91st Street
799-1818
205 East 85th Street
439-8500
897 Broadway at 19th Street
780-9300

The Equinox clubs offer very limited pre- and postnatal exercise classes but recommend using a personal trainer who is certified in pre- and postnatal fitness to work with you to develop a safe and effective exercise program. You must be a member of the club to hire a trainer, and the cost is not included in the membership fee. Ask for the personal training manager at any of the clubs. Equinox is known for its outstanding instructors and offers a wide range of exercise classes. And their locker rooms are immaculate. Baby-sitting is not available.

Maternal Fitness

108 East 16th Street, 4th floor

353-1947

Founded by Julie Tupler, this is a unique fitness program that employs certified personal trainers who are also registered nurses to work one-on-one or in small groups with pregnant women. Sessions are ninety minutes and include stretching and massage. They are sold in groups of five one-on-one sessions for $345. Six group sessions cost $160. The one-on-ones are conducted in your home (Kelly took five sessions at the end of her pregnancy and found them very helpful), while the group workshops (two basic foundation classes, four exercise classes) are held at various locations in the city. Julie is author of the book, *Maternal Fitness: Preparing for a Healthy Pregnancy, an Easier Labor, and a Quick Recovery.*

Motherwell Maternity Health & Fitness

Lenox Hill Hospital/Black Hall

130 East 77th Street

434-2238

Motherwell offers pre- and postnatal fitness classes to all women (not just those delivering at Lenox Hill) for a fee of $85 for the first month (eight classes), and $65 for each additional month. Postpartum classes are Monday and Wednesday from 10 A.M. to 11:30 A.M.; prenatal classes are Monday and Wednesday from 5:30 P.M. to 7 P.M. and Tuesday and Thursday from 10 A.M. to 11:30 A.M. Call to confirm.

New York Health & Racquet Club

110 West 56th Street 541-7200

1433 York Ave. at 76th Street 737-6666

20 East 50th Street 593-1500

132 East 45th Street 986-3100

24 East 13th Street 924-4600

39 Whitehall Street 269-9800

New York Health & Racquet Clubs offer prenatal classes at some of the clubs as need arises. Nicole Korron (737-6666) does the scheduling; call and she will let you know where and when classes are available. NYHRC offers baby-sitting at the York Avenue location only.

New York Sports Clubs

61 West 62nd Street 265-0995

248 West 80th Street 873-1500

1601 Broadway at 49th Street

(Crowne Plaza Hotel) 977-8880

151 East 86th Street 860-8630

575 Lexington Avenue at 51st Street
317-9400

380 Madison Avenue at 46th Street
983-0303

404 Fifth Avenue at 37th Street 594-3120

614 Second Avenue at 34th Street 213-5999

151 Reade Street at Greenwich Street
571-1000

New York Sports Clubs have pre- and postnatal fitness classes and frequent seminars for pregnant women, designed to teach basic fitness guidelines. Lectures cover topics such as stretching, flexibility, and exercise limitations during pregnancy. Prenatal exercise classes are taught by trainers from Maternal Fitness for an additional charge. Many of the clubs located in residential areas offer baby-sitting for a nominal fee. There are fifty locations in New York, so call if you need to find one closer to you. Classes run all day long.

Peggy Levine
212 West 92nd Street
362-5176

Peggy Levine is a well-known name in women's fitness, and her classes are reputed to be excellent. Both pre- and postnatal classes (sixty-five minutes each) are offered for $14 per class. A baby-sitting service ($2 to $3 per child/per class) is also available. Call ahead if you require baby-sitting.

Plus One Fitness Clinic
301 Park Avenue at 49th Street
355-3000, ext. 4970

One World Financial Center
200 Liberty Street 945-2525

New York Hilton
1335 Sixth Avenue at 53rd Street
261-5903

Plus One is a personal-training center, no classes. Prices range from $26 to $75 a visit, depending on the length and type of training. Staff trainers certified in pre- and postnatal fitness offer both one-on-one training and cross training. No baby-sitting is available. There are approximately ten locations, so call for the one nearest you.

Reebok Sports Club
160 Columbus Avenue at 67th Street
362-6800

Reebok offers low-impact water aerobic classes and has personal trainers who specialize in working with women during and after their pregnancies. Once your baby is six months old, you can leave him in the state-of-the-art Kids Club while you exercise. On Sundays, Mommy and Daddy and Me classes are held throughout the day. This is probably the largest and most expensive health club in the city; a yearly membership costs nearly $2,000.

Vertical Club
350 West 50th Street 265-9400
139 West 32nd Street 465-1750
335 Madison Avenue at 43rd Street
983-5320
330 East 61st Street 355-5100

The East 61st Street location offers ninety minute prenatal exercise classes, taught by Diane Gospel, a specialist in training pregnant women. Kelly took these classes religiously, with excellent results. You must be a club member to take classes. No baby-sitting is offered.

YM-YWHA
1395 Lexington Avenue at 92nd Street
415-5729

A prenatal class here (dance/stretching/yoga) is ninety minutes. The cost is $14 per

class for the whole session (fifteen to nineteen weeks) or $16 for each individual class. The postnatal class is seventy-five minutes, for the same price. You must be a member of the Fitness Center to take classes, approximately $700 a year. Baby-sitting is available for a nominal fee.

McBurney YMCA
215 West 23rd Street 741-9210

McBurney offers Moms in Motion, a prenatal exercise class that meets twice a week. Each class is fifty minutes long and includes aerobic exercise and stretching. The cost is $59 per month.

Vanderbilt YMCA
224 East 47th Street 756-9600

The Vanderbilt location offers a forty-five-minute prenatal exercise class, which includes a combination of aerobics and stretch/tone exercises. Classes are held twice a week; an eleven-week series is $120.

YWCA
610 Lexington Avenue at 53rd Street
755-4500

The YWCA offers a Swim Through

Pregnancy class once a week that can be taken for thirty minutes or an hour. The class is a combination of water aerobics and stretching. Price is $110 for eight one-hour sessions, and $60 for eight thirty-minute sessions.

Private Trainers

Here are a few who offer pre- and postnatal private training at your home, gym, or office: Hunter Manuel, 579-9339; Jane Kornbluh, 677-6165; Stephanie Heller, 691-6017; and Anna Puschila, 355-3109. Their fees range from $45 to $60 per hour.

YOGA

Yoga is great for pregnant women—it's relaxing, it helps maintain flexibility, and it's an excellent way to exercise without risking injury.

Many health clubs have yoga classes. If you have taken yoga during your pre-pregnant days and want to continue, do so. Tell your instructor that you're pregnant, and discuss which moves or positions you should not be doing now. As with any kind of exercise, listen to your body—if something feels uncomfortable, don't do it. Ask your instructor for alternatives that will be more comfortable and safer for you.

Yoga instructor Gayatri Martin tells us that prenatal yoga emphasizes the strengthening of pelvic floor muscles to get them ready for pregnancy and birth. This class also allows more time than traditional yoga for resting and relaxation. You'll learn helpful breathing and postures for birth and labor.

The following yoga instructors or studios specialize in pre- and postnatal yoga classes:

Mary Ryan Barnes
175 West 93rd Street
222-8597

Mary, a certified yoga instructor, teaches classes for pregnant women at various facilities, including Peggy Levine and Urban Yoga Workout. She also will conduct private yoga classes in your home or hers for $60 per session.

Integral Yoga Center
227 West 13th Street
929-0586

The Integral Yoga Center offers a multitude of classes for all levels, including prenatal yoga, at various times throughout the week. Each class is ninety minutes. A single class is $8; ten classes are $70; and twenty classes are $130.

Peggy Levine

214 West 92nd Street

749-1378

Peggy's class is offered once a week for sixty-five minutes and costs $14. A baby-sitter is provided during some classes for $2 to $3, per class, per child. Call twenty-four hours ahead if you need a sitter.

Mikelle Terson

37 West 76th Street

362-4288

Mikelle has been teaching yoga for two years at the Reebok Sports Club and Chelsea Piers. She is available for private sessions at your home for $125 per seventy-five-minute session.

Christine Wade

462 Greenwich Street

226-5194

Christine teaches at the Integral Yoga Center and gives private lessons. Her unique classes include Yoga for Labor and Herbs for Pregnancy. Christine is the president of ICAN/NY and is a terrific resource for alternative birth practitioners.

MASSAGE

Many women suffer from back pain and strain, especially during the later months of their pregnancy. Massage can help.

When looking for a massage therapist, make sure he or she is licensed by New York State. Ask if she has been certified in prenatal massage, or has experience working with pregnant women. Your massage therapist should be attuned to the physical changes in the pregnant body and skilled at using massage to relieve aches and tension in the areas that are causing the most discomfort—usually the lower back and shoulder muscles.

Communication with your therapist is critical. If you feel lightheaded, short of breath, or uncomfortable at all during your massage, let the practitioner know. Many women feel uncomfortable lying on their backs after the fourth month (ACOG recommends that you do not lie on your back after this time), so prenatal massages are often given to a woman lies on her side with pillows between her legs. The

Medical Massage Group has a special table with a cut-out middle so that you can lie on your stomach when you might be uncomfortable on your side.

The massage therapists listed here have all worked with pregnant women; some specialize in prenatal massage, and many will come to your home for an additional fee. All work by appointment only, so call ahead.

Barbara Close*
2095 Broadway
873-7966

Prenatal massage is $65 for seventy minutes. Pamela swears by Barbara and used her especially to ease sore lower back muscles toward the end of her pregnancy.

Carapan
5 West 16th Street
633-6220

Carapan is a Zen-like massage center, with some practitioners experienced in prenatal massage. The atmosphere here is sublime—extremely peaceful. Fees are $45 for thirty minutes and $75 for one hour.

Laura Favin
324 W. 89th Street
501-0606

Laura has been giving massages for over ten years—and uses lots of pillows. She charges $60 for a one-hour massage, $85 if she travels to your home or office.

The Quiet Touch
various locations throughout the city
246-0008

Massage therapists here are trained by the Swedish Massage Institute, and many have additional training in prenatal massage. The Quiet Touch maintains suites across the city and provides an address only after you've made an appointment. You'll pay $40 for thirty minutes; $70 for one hour; home sessions are available for slightly more.

Elaine Stillerman
108 East 16th Street, 4th floor
533-3188

Elaine has been practicing Mother-Massage for more than fifteen years and is the author of MotherMassage: A Handbook for Relieving the Discomforts of Pregnancy.

She is on staff at the Swedish Institute of Massage. Her rate for a massage is $70 per hour.

The Medical Massage Group*
1556 York Ave. at 83rd Street
472-4772

Donna and Harvey Manger-Weil, Kelly's personal favorite, are wonderful, and they have created a warm and peaceful environment in their home. Harvey's reflexology has helped many women with morning sickness. With a unique massage table that allows even a woman in her ninth month to lie comfortably on her stomach, it is no wonder that seventy percent of their practice is pregnancy massage. Fees are $75 for one hour in their office, $40 for one-half hour, and $100 for one hour at your home.

NUTRITION

You know that good nutrition is a critical part of producing a healthy baby, and there are many books available addressing this subject. *What to Expect When You're Expecting*, the pregnancy bible, has an excellent section called the "Best Odds Diet," with guidelines on how to eat every day; and *What to Eat When You're Expecting*. Your OB or CNM will probably talk to you about nutrition too, but if he doesn't, bring it up yourself.

In some cases—if you are underweight, overweight, diabetic or need extra help managing your diet—talk to a nutritionist to set up a diet that meets your needs. The American Board of Nutrition (9650 Rockville Pike, Bethesda, MD 20014; 301-530-7110) can provide you with a listing of board-certified nutritionists with M.D.s or Ph.D.s in your area. Send a self-addressed stamped envelope to the American Board of Nutrition. Weight Watchers also offers a healthy plan for overweight pregnant women.

Eating Right While You're Pregnant

Here are some important facts to know about nutrition and pregnancy:

Eat regularly and well. This is no time to diet. You *will* gain weight, and most obstetricians today say a gain of twenty-five, thirty-five, or even more pounds is normal and healthy. You should increase your calorie intake—by about 300 calories a day during

the last two trimesters—because you need more energy during this time.

* Eat healthy foods. That means ample daily servings of grains (cereal, whole grain bread, crackers), fruits, vegetables (steamed are best), protein (eggs, meat, fish, peanut butter), and calcium (milk, cheese, yogurt, tofu).

* Avoid junk food. You do need extra calories, but make them good, nutrient-rich calories. When you want sugar, reach for the fresh fruit. Fruit is sweet, nutritious, and will help you avoid the ubiquitous affliction of pregnancy, constipation.

* Drink water. To maintain body fluids and keep yourself cooled off while you're pregnant (your core body temperature is higher now than normal), you need to take in lots of liquids, at least two quarts a day. Milk and juice are good for you; water is always great, especially before, during and after exercise.

* Do not drink alcohol.

* Don't drink caffeinated beverages (coffee, tea, colas) during your first trimester, and restrict your intake of those beverages to one or perhaps two cups a day after that. Caffeine can reach the baby through the placenta.

* Listen to your body. Some of those famous cravings may have a basis in physiology. If you have a powerful and unexpected yen for a bag of potato chips, go for it—your body may need a little added salt.

The following nutritionists have all worked with pregnant women. Initial consultations cost around $100, with follow-up visits ranging from $35 to $75. You can also call the American Dietetic Association for certified dietitian nutritionists (C.D.N.) in your area. The consumer hotline for referrals is 900-225-5267.

Erica Ilton, R.D., C.D.N.
529-0654

Elyse Sosin, R.D.
289-1197

Annette Warpeha-Adams. R.D.
772-0901

Joanne Diamond, R.D.
982-0371

Bonnie Taub-Dix, M.A., R.D., C.D.N.
Practices in New York City and Long Island: 737-8536; 516-295-0377

3 · from health care to day care

Sometime toward the end of your pregnancy, you will begin to search for the people who will help you care for your little one. This is a toughie. The very idea of entrusting your baby to someone else is scary. You'll feel more comfortable if you take the time to do the initial legwork—scout around, ask questions, make phone calls, pay visits.

First, you will need to find a pediatrician. Your goal is to find one you and your husband/partner connect with, who will see to it that your baby receives the best available care.

You may wish to hire a baby nurse or doula to help out in your home the first few days or weeks after your baby is born. After that, your child-care needs will depend on what else is going on in your life. If you're returning to a job after a maternity leave, you'll probably require full-time help, either in your home or outside of it. If you work at home or are involved in activities that will take you away from your child for some hours each day or week, you'll be looking for child care on a part-time basis. And if you just want to get out of the house from time to time, sans baby, it will be handy to have one or two reliable baby-sitters listed in your phone book. If you have extended family nearby, you may be lucky enough to have some occasional free baby-sitting coming your way.

In this chapter, we'll show you how to find reliable child care. We'll give you names and numbers and our own impressions to help you get the ball rolling.

PEDIATRICIANS

You should begin looking for a pediatrician during the last few months of your pregnancy. Your baby's doctor will be noted on the record form that your obstetrician will send to the hospital about a month prior to your due date, and the pediatrician will then come by the hospital to examine your baby.

Here's how to find one, and what you should look for:

Ask your obstetrician for a recommendation. If your doctor lives in the city, who does she use for her own children?

✳ Ask relatives, neighbors, and friends about pediatricians they use.

✳ Call any of the hospitals in the city, and ask for a referral from the pediatric department.

✳ Go to the New York Public Library and look up listings in the American Academy of Pediatrics Directory.

✳ Consider location. Your newborn will be going to the doctor often, and having a pediatrician with an office near your home is more practical, especially during an emergency or a spell of nasty weather.

✳ Consider whether you place importance on the doctor's age, type of practice (group, partnership, or solo practitioner), or gender (some parents prefer to have a pediatrician the same sex as their baby).

Once you have the names of two or three pediatricians who sound promising, call their offices and set up a consultation. Most will agree to make appointments in the early evening after regular office hours. Any good doctor should be willing to take the time to meet with you and your husband/partner. Kelly requested consultations with five pediatricians. One did not conduct prenatal interviews; the other four were happy to meet with her and her husband to answer questions and give them a brief office tour. (If your prospective pediatrician is part of a group practice, it's a good idea to meet with all the doctors, if possible, because chances are each one will be treating your child at one time or another.)

We suggest preparing a list of questions in advance and writing down the doctors' answers. That way, you can compare pediatricians and discuss everything with your husband/partner if he can't be with you at each consultation. While you are waiting to talk with your prospective pediatrician, look around the waiting room.

Is it child friendly, with enough toys, pictures, and books to keep a baby or toddler busy during a wait to see the doctor?

* Is the receptionist friendly, or does she seem curt and harried?

* If you're visiting during office hours, ask parents in the waiting room about their experiences with the doctor you are about to meet.

* Find out how long they typically wait to see the doctor. A forty-five minute wait with a sick toddler is no fun.

* Do sick and healthy children wait in the same waiting room? Kelly's pediatrician has eight examination rooms, and babies under a year old automatically go into one of these. The office tries to keep only healthy children in the waiting area.

When you sit down with the doctor, ask:

How does the doctor answer parents' non-emergency calls throughout the day? Is there a call-in hour or does the doctor take calls all day and return them intermittently between patients? Is there a nurse who can answer questions?

* How are emergencies handled? Is the doctor affiliated with a nearby hospital? Is the practice affiliated with more than one hospital?

* How does the pediatrician feel about breast-feeding? If you plan to breastfeed, you will want a pediatrician who is supportive and encouraging.

* What are the pediatrician's views on circumcision, nutrition, immunizations, and preventive medicine? It is important that you and your doctor are in sync on most of these issues.

If you don't feel rushed during the consultation, and the pediatrician is patient with you, these are good indicators of how the doctor will be with your baby. Again, don't be afraid to ask any questions.

BABY NURSES/ DOULAS

Immediately after the birth of your baby, you may wish to have a baby nurse or doula.

Baby nurses usually come the day you bring the baby home and live with you in your apartment for a week or two or longer. An in-home nurse works twenty-four hours a day, seven days a week. She cares for the baby, gets up in the middle of the night to change and feed him or bring him to you for breast-feeding, and generally allows you to sleep late and rest up.

Baby nurses are expensive, costing from $125 to $160 a day. Some will live-out and work for shorter periods (not a full day).

A doula comes to your home for a few hours each day and almost always lives-out. She helps and pampers you: she does the grocery shopping, laundry, and fixes meals, so you will have more time with your baby. She may also assist you in taking care of your baby by bathing or changing him, and she should be able to answer questions regarding breastfeeding.

When you hire a doula, typically you buy a set block of visits or hours with a fifteen-hour minimum. Each visit is at least three hours, costing approximately $24 an hour.

The best way to find a baby nurse or doula is through a trusted friend who has used one herself. Or, call one of the many agencies that have baby nurse divisions. Kelly hired her nurse, Olga, through an agency and was extremely pleased. Olga had been taking care of babies for more than twenty years, and her references were impeccable. She is so good, in fact, that one family kept her for five years!

An agency will send three or four candidates for you to interview while you are pregnant. You may then reserve the baby nurse or doula of your choice, and the agency will try not to place her for two weeks around your due date. If you are late or early, the nurse you've requested may be on another job, but this rarely happens. Agencies are very good at monitoring their baby nurses' schedules.

Baby nurses get booked way in advance, so plan early. Kelly started asking friends for recommendations when she was five months pregnant, and three of the names she received were already booked.

Of course, your mother or mother-in-law may offer to come stay with you or may insist on it. If you feel comfortable with a family member living in and helping out, great. However, we've found that many new parents prefer to hire short-term professional help which allows them to get the rest they need without having to impose on—or be nice to—a relative.

The following is a list of baby nurse and doula agencies in the New York area. We have had personal experiences with Avalon and In a Family Way, and found the owners of these two agencies to be caring, responsible, and trustworthy.

Avalon Registry*
162 West 56th Street, Suite 507
245-0250

Beyond Birth (Doulas)
3635 Hill Boulevard, Suite #123
Jefferson Valley, NY 10535
914-245-2229

Bohne's Baby Nursing
16 East 79th Street, Suite G-4
879-7920

Doula Care
Ruth Callahan
70 West 93rd Street 749-6613

Foley Nursing Agency
799 Madison Avenue 794-9666

Fox Agency
30 East 60th Street 753-2686

In a Family Way*
124 West 79th Street, Suite 9-B
877-8112

Mother Nurture
Doula Service
P.O. Box 284
Glen Oaks, NY 11004
718-631-BABY (718-631-2229)

Plaza Nurses Agency
50 Broadway
Lynbrook, NY 11563
(516-466-1662)

NANNIES

Hiring someone to look after your child while you're at work or away is stressful and nerve-racking. You want someone who is good, kind, smart, honest, sober, reliable, loves kids, knows infant CPR, bakes cookies, and is going to think your baby is the most adorable child she's ever seen. You want another you.

You won't find another you, but if you're determined and dogged and keep your ears open, you will locate someone who will be an affectionate, caring, responsible child care provider for your youngster. Kelly conducted her own nanny search during the writing of this chapter, so we can offer the up-to-date experiences of a New York mother looking for good child care.

You may want a nanny who lives with you or one who comes to your home each morning and leaves each evening. You may need this person's help on a part-time or full-time basis. There are several ways to go about finding her. As is true for so many services, word of mouth is the best place to start. Ask friends who have child care whether their nannies have friends looking for work. When we were in search of help, we stopped nannies in the park, talked to mothers and nan-

Top Ten Things to Look For in a Caregiver

1. References. And strong ones!
2. The ability to speak and read English or your native language.
3. Personality—it's hard to be around someone who never smiles.
4. Experience—especially with children the same age as your own.
5. Honesty—if she lies about her age, what else will she lie about?
6. Patience.
7. Positive attitude.
8. Nice appearance.
9. Reliability and responsibility.
10. Instinct—trust your own feelings.

nies at the classes we took with our children, and looked at bulletin board notices in child- and religious-oriented institutions. Many schools as well as the Parent's League also post nanny information on bulletin boards.

If you get nowhere by word of mouth, try the newspapers. Many parents have successfully found child care by advertising in newspapers or by answering an ad. We'll show you how to do that shortly. Finally, a number of agencies specialize in nanny placement. We list those agencies below.

However you come by your candidates, we cannot stress enough the importance of checking references and thoroughly questioning them. On more than one occasion, we have heard stories of falsified references in which nannies listed friends instead of former employers. Toward the end of this section, we'll give you a list of some of the most important questions to ask your future nanny and her references. You may also want to read *How to Hire A Nanny* by Elaine S. Pelletier. This step-by-step guide helps you through the nanny search. Full-time (five days a week), live-out nannies usually start at around $300 a week and can go as high as $500 for an experienced, educated caregiver. Live-in nannies, for whom you provide room and board, usually start at $200 to $250.

Newspaper Advertisements

Placing a classified ad can be an excellent way to find a nanny. The *Irish Echo*, the *Irish Voice*, and *The New York Times* are popular nanny-finding papers. A number of newspapers are published for various nationalities and many nannies look in them for jobs. There is a German paper, a Polish paper, and an Italian paper, for example. Explore them if you would prefer a nanny from a specific country, when you would like your child to learn a foreign language or if your spouse is from another country.

When you place an ad, be as specific as possible to limit your responses. If you must have a nonsmoker, live-in help, or someone with a driver's license, say so. If you need someone to work on Saturdays or stay late in the evening, state it. Check the classified sections to see examples of help-wanted ads or follow our example:

Upper East Side Nanny Needed.
Live-in nanny needed for a two-year-old boy. Light housekeeping, shopping, and errands. Must have two years experience with toddlers and excellent references. Nonsmoker. Must swim, drive, and cook. Must have legal working papers. M–F, weekends off. Own room, TV-VCR, A/C. Call 555-5555.

When Kelly ran an ad similar to this one in two newspapers three weeks before Christmas, she received more than two hundred phone calls. In fact, her phone began ringing at 6 A.M. the Wednesday morning the *Irish Echo* came out and by 11 A.M. she had received sixty calls.

Interview candidates on the phone before you bring them to your home. Tell them about the job, find out what they are looking for, and ask about their past work experience. Kelly needed a caregiver who could work on Saturdays and travel with the family, and she was able to eliminate, over the phone, a number of candidates who could not fill those requirements.

We recommend making a list of the three most appealing and the three least appealing aspects of your job. Discuss them with the applicant over the phone. Start with the three worst aspects: she must arrive at 7:30 every morning, she will be alone with the baby all day, and she will be expected to do grocery shopping and some meal preparation. If the applicant is still interested and if you are pleased with her responses to your key questions, proceed from there with an interview in your home or office.

The following four newspapers are reliable and frequently used. When you call, check on the listing deadlines. Ads can be phoned or faxed, using a credit card.

Irish Echo

309 Fifth Avenue New York, NY 10016
686-1266

The *Irish Echo* comes out once a week on Wednesdays. Ads must be submitted before 11 A.M. the Friday before the ad is to run. Three lines cost $15 and each additional line is $4.

Irish Voice

323 Fifth Avenue New York, NY 10016
686-3366

The *Irish Voice* comes out Wednesdays and accepts ads up to the previous Monday. Thirty words cost approximately $29.

The New York Times

229 West 43rd St. New York, NY 10036
354-3900

An ad placed in the classified section of *The New York Times* can run in the Sunday edition only or in the Sunday edition plus two weekdays. Four lines on Sunday costs $106; Sunday and two weekdays costs $178; and four lines for a week costs $316.

The Polish Daily News

Nowy Dziennik

333 West 38th Street New York, NY 10018

594-2266, ext. 31

This daily paper (except Sundays) is written in Polish, but many of the classifieds are in English. Ads must be submitted by noon to run in the next day's paper. A thirty-five word ad running for one week costs $50; for Monday through Wednesday, $10; on Thursday or Friday, $12; and on Saturday, $14.

Agencies

The more people they place, the more money agencies make, so high turnover is beneficial to their business. This is contrary to what you are looking for—someone who will stay with you a long time. Also, although agencies claim they check references, many have been known to send a candidate on an interview with skimpy or weak references. Be cautious if, for example, a nanny's previous employer has moved and now has an unlisted phone number somewhere in Florida, or if the applicant hands you a hand-written letter of reference with grammatically incorrect sentences and misspelled words.

Although we can't personally endorse any of the agencies listed below, we know people who have found good help through them. We suggest you read the Department of Consumer Affairs' forty-two-page report on placement agencies entitled, "Who's Watching Our Kids?" You can write to the Department of Consumer Affairs, 42 Broadway, New York, NY 10004, and request a copy. The report lists fifty agencies investigated by the department and any violations filed against them. You can also call their office, at 487-4444, to check whether a particular agency is licensed, whether it has received any complaints, or to file a complaint yourself.

A Choice of Nanny

130 West 57th Street New York, NY 10019

246-KIDS (246-5437)

Best Domestic Services Agency

10 East 39th Street New York, NY 10016

685-0351

The Fox Agency

30 East 60th Street New York, NY 10022

753-2686

Frances Stuart Agency

1220 Lexington Avenue at 83rd Street

New York, NY 10028 439-9222

Domestically Yours

535 Fifth Avenue at 44th Street

New York, NY 10017 986-1900

The London Agency

767 Lexington Avenue at 60th Street

New York, NY 10021 755-5064

Nannies Plus

520 Speedwell Avenue, Suite 114

Morris Plains, NJ 07950 800-752-0078

NY Nanny Center

31 Bayles Avenue

Port Washington, NY 11050

516-767-5136

Professional Nannies Institute

501 Fifth Avenue at 43rd Street

New York, NY 10016 692-9510

Robin Kellner Agency

221 West 57th St. New York, NY 10019

247-4141

Town and Country

157 West 57th St. New York, NY 10019

245-8400

Finally, the Irish Center in the Bronx helps Irish immigrants find nanny work. The center does not screen applicants, but acts as a referral service at no charge. They will take down your job requirements and have aplicants contact you. Most nannies want live-out positions. Call the center at 718-882-8520.

The Interview

Nothing is as important as the interview to determine whether a candidate is the right person to take care of your little one. Be conscious of the atmosphere you create. Are you interviewing potential nannies at your office, in your formal living room, in the playroom, family room, or at the kitchen table? Are you looking for someone to join the family, or will this person be more of an employee with a formal working arrangement?

Here's our suggested list of interview questions:

Tell me about yourself. Where are you from? Where did you grow up?

* Why do you want to be a nanny? What is it you like about being a nanny?

* What previous child-care experience do you have? Tell me about those jobs.

* What was a typical day like? What did your duties/responsibilities include? (Look for someone who has held a child-care position

similar to the one you are offering. If she cooked and cleaned on the last job and you are looking for light cooking and cleaning, she won't be upset if you ask her to grill a chicken breast or wipe off the kitchen counter.)

❋ How many children did you take care of in your previous positions? How old were they?

❋ Do you have children of your own?

❋ What did you like best about your previous job? What did you like least?

❋ Why did you leave your last job(s)?

❋ Do you smoke?

❋ Do you have CPR or first-aid training ?

❋ Can you stay late during the week or work on weekends if necessary?

❋ How have you handled emergencies or stressful situations in your past jobs? Describe one.

❋ What are your child-rearing philosophies and views on discipline? Do you believe in spanking and time-outs?

❋ What are your interests? What do you like to do when you're not working?

❋ Do you have any health restrictions or dietary preferences I should know about?

❋ What are you looking for in a family?

❋ Would you travel with the family if needed?

❋ Do you know your way around the city?

❋ When could you start? What are your salary requirements?

Checking References

Checking references with previous employers can be one of the most challenging parts of the child-care process. Who are you calling? How can you be sure the name you have been given is not a candidate's friend or relative? And then, some people just aren't very talkative on the telephone.

Use your common sense and intuition; be open and friendly; and identify yourself in detail. For example: "Hello Mrs. X, this is Mrs. Y, and I am calling to check a reference on Susan Jones, who told me she worked for you. My husband and I live in New York City on East 53rd Street and we have a three-year-old daughter." Tell her a little about your family. This will help break the ice and allow you to ask about her family and work situations. It's important to know the kind of household in which your potential nanny has worked, because it may be very different from your own. If Mrs. X had a staff of three, and Susan had no household duties, she may not be happy in your home if you ask her to cook, clean, and do the laundry. Be realistic.

Here are some questions you may want to ask:

How long was Susan with you?

❋ Why did she leave?

❋ How many children do you have? How old are they?

❋ What were Susan's responsibilities?

❋ Do you work? What do you do? Were either you or your husband at home during the day or was Susan pretty much on her own?

❋ What were her hours?

❋ Was there ever an emergency or difficult situation that Susan had to handle on her own?

❋ How would you describe her overall personality and attitude?

❋ How did you meet Susan?

❋ Was it easy to communicate with her? Did she give you feedback on your children? Did she take direction/instruction well?

❋ Did she cook, clean, drive, run errands, swim, iron (or whatever you need most)?

❋ Did you trust her? Did you find her reliable and honest?

❋ How did your children like her?

❋ Would you hire her again?

Several agencies verify references on nannies. Nanny Check (800-742-3316) investigates driving violations, criminal records, and employment references. They also confirm academic degrees, old addresses, club, or group memberships. They charge $50 for each reference and $35 to check for criminal convictions in a single county.

American International Security (703-691-1110) has a one-price fee, $75, for which you obtain a motor vehicle record, a New York City criminal convictions record, and a credit report, as well as a verification of social security number, previous addresses, and places of employment.

When the Nanny Starts

After you have found the right person, it is important to watch how she and your baby interact in order to make sure they are comfortable with each other. It's a good idea to have prepared a typewritten list of duties as well as what is expected of the nanny on a daily basis, aside from child-care, such as cooking, cleaning, laundry, grocery shopping. Be specific. Sit down and go over everything within the first few days to make sure she understands the responsibilities of the job. Set a date for a follow-up meeting in two weeks to discuss how things are going, what's working well, and any areas of difficulty.

You may also want your nanny to have a physical examination. Certainly, inquire about her health and vaccinations. Depending on where your nanny is from and how long she has been in this country, she may not be vaccinated against measles, mumps and rubella, or chicken pox. If she's not, arrange with your doctor for her to get these shots.

Once a nanny is on the job, you may want to monitor her activities in your absence. Parents who have had to hire a caregiver very quickly and have little time to train and supervise may find that this service provides peace of mind: In Home Nanny Surveillance can be reached at 886-4882; P.O. Box 2162, Rockefeller Station, New York, NY 10185.

Care Check, created by Lori Berke and Gail Cohen, is another service which offers videotaping as a learning tool for better communication between you and your caregiver. Care Check can help you with the prescreening process, including interview techniques and questions, and they will (for $175) conduct a check on your applicant, confirming previous employment, education, passport, and other records. International credit checks may cost more. Care Check has state of the art equipment and will rent or sell any customized surveillance system you need. A two-day video surveillance rental costs $200. Care Check can be reached at 360-6640; 1056 Fifth Avenue, New York, NY 10028.

Baby Watch, a nationwide, service similar to Care Check, has been in business for six years. The New York provider is Lori Schechter. She will install a monitoring device in your home to evaluate your nanny's performance. The cost is approximately $250 for a two-day rental. Lori also provides her clients an comprehensive guide for hiring a nanny. Baby Watch can be reached at 889-1494.

Taxes and Insurance

Remember that once you hire a nanny, you have become an employer. According to CPA Stuart Rosenblum, writing in *New York Magazine* in 1995, you must:

1. **Apply for an employer identification number with the IRS using form SS-4.**
2. **File schedule H, a new tax form that replaces the old form 942. Employers report wages paid to household workers or nannies**

on their income tax returns. Schedule H, which is filed with your 1040, simplifies the work of calculating social security, Medicare, and federal income taxes.

3. Each year, give your nanny a W-2 form, listing total wages and taxes paid, by January 31.

4. File a W-3, a summary of all your W-2s, by February 28. File quarterly and annual state reports.

Other forms to fill out include federal unemployment and state unemployment tax forms. These cover anyone who earns more than $100 a quarter. The federal unemployment tax form 940 can be obtained from the IRS; the New York State Labor Department supplies state unemployment forms.

Other areas of concern are compensation and disability policies. If you employ a child-care provider for more than forty hours a week, you should buy a workers' compensation and disability policy. These start at around $300. Call the State Insurance Fund for more information (312-9000). The IRS publishes two booklets to help employers through this maze: "Employment Taxes for Household Employers" (Book 926) and "What You Need to Know If You Hire Domestic Help" (Book 27). To receive these booklets, call 800-462-8100. Call the New York State Department of Labor (718-797-7032) to request the "Employer's Guide to Unemployment Insurance." Good luck!

AU PAIRS

Hiring an au pair is a child-care option many parents find practical and economical.

Au pairs come to the United States from various countries, usually European. They can remain in this country legally for one year and work a forty-five-hour week. Generally, an au pair has a week-long orientation just after she arrives in this country, and takes one academic course during her stay. In addition, she is provided with support counselors and a health plan by her umbrella organization.

An au pair lives with you and is paid between $115 and $200 a week. You can interview a prospective au pair over the phone, and most agencies provide background information on several candidates.

Au pairs tend to be inexperienced child care providers. They most often work in homes with stay-at-home mothers. They are not allowed to remain alone with children overnight, so an au pair is not a good option for parents who travel.

If you are interested in an au pair, contact the following agencies:

Au Pair America
102 Greenwich Avenue
Greenwich, CT 06830
800-9au-pair (800-928-7247)

Au Pair/Homestay
(part of the Experiment
in International Living)
1015 15 Street NW, Suite 750
Washington, DC 20005 202-408-5380

Au Pair USA/Interexchange
161 Sixth Avenue New York, NY 10013
800-Au-Pairs (800-287-2477)

Au Pair Childcrest
6985 Union Park Center, Suite 340
Salt Lake City, UT 84047 (800-574-8889)

DAY CARE CENTERS

New York City has more than 2,500 day care centers, where you can bring your child each morning and pick him up no later than 6 P.M. Centers must be licensed by the State of New York and meet rigid requirements.

One of the most professionally run day care centers we know is the Bright Horizons Center at 435 East 70th Street (746-6543). This nationwide chain has an excellent reputation as a leader in upholding stringent day care standards. In addition, there are approximately 5,300 in-home care centers or family day care providers in the city. In family day care, an individual takes care of a few children (by law, no more than twelve) in her home. The provider must be licensed by New York State and must register with the Department of Health. Even so, be cautious. Pay a personal visit to the center, speak with other parents, and trust your instincts.

Also investigate options offered by your employer. More and more companies are offering on-site day care or are willing to contribute to day care costs.

To learn more about what's available, contact the following:

The Department of Health is the city agency that regulates day care centers and will tell you whether a specific center is licensed. Call 334-7814, and ask for the day care bureau.

✳ **The Daycare Council of New York refers up to**

twenty-five centers, free of charge. Centers are printed out by zip code, and you can request referrals in three zip codes. The Daycare Council of New York is located at 10 East 34th Street, New York, NY 10016. Their phone number is 213-2423. You probably want to look at centers that are in your home and office zip codes to compare and contrast.

✳ Child Care Inc., located at 275 Seventh Avenue, New York, NY 10001, 929-4999, is a nonprofit organization that serves as an information and referral resource for New York parents. Their excellent guides include "Choosing Child Care for Your Infant or Toddler," "Choosing an Early Childhood Program," and "In-Home Care." Other handouts cover finding and working with in-home care or nanny agencies, and they have samples of a model contract for household employment. Child Care will also prepare lists of day care and in-home care by zip code.

✳ The Library for Child Development (718-260-2000) provides information on 370 subsidized day care centers and 170 Head Start Centers in New York City.

BABY-SITTING

You may be a stay-at-home mom who requires only a little child care on a Saturday night or a few afternoons a week. The solution here is a baby-sitter. Ask your doorman, superintendent, or neighbor whether there are teenagers in the building available for baby-sitting, or check out colleges that have baby-sitting services or a baby-sitting agency. Each service works differently; often there is an initial registration fee between $15 and $45. Many require a two-hour minimum and have varying rates, starting at $6 an hour. Look for a sitter who has experience with children the same age as your child, and check references. Don't assume that just because someone is enrolled in a local college she is trustworthy.

Finally, tell everyone you know that you're looking for a sitter. Ask other baby-sitters or nannies for recommendations; check bulletin boards at your pediatrician's office and play spaces. Pamela uses Barnard Baby-Sitting Service and finds the students always reliable and competent.

The following is a list of baby-sitting services and placement offices at local colleges.

BABY-SITTING SERVICES

Barnard Baby-Sitting Service/
Barnard College 854-2035

Pinch Sitters 260-6005

Baby-Sitting Guild 682-0227

Beth Israel School of Nursing 614-6110
(Will post jobs on bulletin board for students.)

COLLEGE PLACEMENT OFFICES

Manhattan

Baruch College 397-1060

Community College 346-8050

Columbia University 854-3804

City College 650-7226

Fashion Institute of Technology 760-7654

Hunter College 772-4849

John Jay College 237-8000

Julliard School 799-5000, ext. 313

Manhattan School of Music 749-2802

Marymount Manhattan College 517-0550

New York University 998-4757

Teachers College, Columbia University
678-3175

This Baby-sitting Service List courtesy of Child Care Inc.

Brooklyn

New York City Technical College
718-722-8848

Brooklyn College 718-951-5696

Kingsborough Community College
718-368-5000

Medgar Evers College 718-270-4900

4 · adjusting to new motherhood

After you bring your newborn home, you will notice that your bulging belly isn't the only thing gone—you'll now be missing all semblance of being organized and in control of your life . . . but that's OK.

The first few weeks at home are going to be turbulent. Like many new mothers, you may feel a bit blue or depressed. Having a baby is an emotionally draining experience, and, to complicate things, those hormones really kick in after the birth. You may feel tired all day. Life may seem reduced to baby feedings, diaper changing, and laundry, laundry, laundry. And order in your apartment will deteriorate at an astonishing rate.

Our advice: Let the place get messy. Use the time between feedings, changes, and naps to take care of yourself—rest and think about what an adorable child you have. Allow willing friends and grandparents to throw in a load of laundry for you or pick up your dry cleaning.

Forget about cooking; order in. New York is take-out heaven, and there is wonderful prepared food all around you. Start to order in other necessities, too. Most pharmacies will take phone orders and deliver. The big drugstore chains, such as Genovese, Duane Reade, Love's, and Rite Aid, all deliver formula by the case and disposable diapers and baby wipes by the

Top Ten Things to Keep You Sane with a Newborn

1. Stock the freezer before the baby is born—lasagna, soup, etc.
2. Get help—a friend, mother, sister, or baby-sitter, if possible. Remember: any relief is better than none.
3. Sleep when the baby sleeps.
4. Order take-out food the first few weeks; it's too tiring to cook.
5. Buy in bulk—a case of formula, a box of diapers, and several packages of baby wipes will make life much easier.
6. Open up charge accounts at stores in the neighborhood that will deliver.
7. Let the house get messy.
8. Make friends with other new moms, and call them.
9. Try to go outside every day.
10. Attend a new mother's luncheon or class.

package. Have your food and supplies delivered from your local supermarket. Make it easy on yourself.

And then, take a class to find out you're not alone. This book gives you dozens of ways to meet new mothers and learn from experts. We also give you hot lines and warm lines to get help at home and some special conveniences only New York can provide.

NEW MOTHER CLASSES

Once your baby is a few weeks old and you have settled into something of a routine, you'll enjoy getting out to swap baby stories with other mothers and to share advice and experiences on how to best care for your infant.

A number of hospitals offer classes you can attend with your baby. They provide an opportunity to hear from pediatricians, child psychologists, child-safety experts, and other skilled professionals. Plus, you'll be able to ask questions and meet other new parents.

When Alexander was six weeks old, Kelly attended the five-week New Mother Discussion Group at New York Hospital. This class, led by Jean Schoppel, R.N. and Ronni Soled, became the highlight of her week. Pamela took the New Mother/New Baby class, for mothers with children newborn to nine months, offered by the 92nd Street Y, and loved it.

We recommend signing up for one of these classes. They are good ways to get information, relieve the isolation you may be feeling during these first weeks with your baby, and talk with other new moms.

Hospital Classes

The hospitals listed below offer new mother classes. Fees vary from hospital to hospital and change frequently; the range is $25 to $50 for one-time classes or workshops, and $120 to $150 for a series of classes or new mother support group meetings. Most hospital classes and support groups are open to all women, not just those who delivered at that hospital. So, if you want to take a class at New York Hospital but deliver at Beth Israel, just call New York Hospital to sign up. New moms are encouraged to bring their babies to all classes.

Beth Israel Hospital
16th Street at First Avenue
420-2000 (General)
420-2999 (Classes)

Beth Israel offers a variety of classes for the new mother, including a CPR course, a class in child safety, a breastfeeding class, and a New Mother's Support Group.

Columbia Presbyterian Hospital
Babies Hospital/Sloane Hospital for Women
Broadway at 166th Street
305-2500 (General)
305-2040 (Parent Education Program)

Columbia Presbyterian offers classes in breastfeeding, baby care, and parenting.

Lenox Hill Hospital
100 East 77th Street
434-2000 (General)
434-2238 (Parent Education Office)

Lenox Hill offers classes in CPR, basic infant care, infant massage, breastfeeding, and has a New Mother's Support Group. They also offer postpartum exercise classes twice a week.

The Mount Sinai Medical Center
One Gustave L. Levy Place
Klingenstein Pavilion
Fifth Avenue at 98th Street
241-6500 (General)
241-7491 (Women & Children's Office)
241-6578 (Breastfeeding Help Line)

Mount Sinai offers classes in caring for newborns, CPR, and breastfeeding, and has a New Mother's Support Group that meets once a week.

New York Hospital/Cornell Medical Center

525 East 68th Street

746-5454 (General)

746-3215 (Preparation for

Parenthood Office)

New York Hospital offers "Adapting to Parenthood," which can be taken before or after a baby is born, and a baby care class. It also has a New Mother's Discussion Group that meets Wednesdays 11 A.M. to 1 P.M. The Preparation for Parenthood staff maintains an information telephone line for new mothers.

New York University Medical Center

560 First Avenue at 32nd Street

263-7200 (General)

263-7201 (Classes)

New York University Medical Center offers a breastfeeding support group for new mothers that meets once a week.

Roosevelt Hospital

1000 Tenth Avenue at 59th Street

523-4000 (General)

523-6222 (Parent/Family Education)

Roosevelt Hospital offers classes in baby care, infant CPR, child CPR, breastfeeding, and has a New Mother's Support Group.

St. Luke's Hospital

1111 Amsterdam Avenue at 114th Street

same phone numbers as Roosevelt Hospital

All classes are given at Roosevelt Hospital.

St. Vincent's Hospital and Medical Center

153 West 11th Street

604-7000 (General)

604-7946 (Maternity Education)

St. Vincent's offers classes in newborn care and breastfeeding and has a Breast-feeding Support Group.

Other Classes, Groups, and Seminars

There are excellent nonhospital-based support/discussion groups throughout the city. Many of them, like the hospital classes, teach infant CPR, which every new parent should learn. Some of the classes listed are fun to take with your child.

Schedules and fees are subject to change. While we have provided some, call for the most up-to-date information.

Baby-Life

201-836-1616

Baby-Life offers a comprehensive three and one-half hour class teaching techniques in CPR, mouth-to-mouth resuscitation, and mini-Heimlich maneuvers for new parents. The fee is $58 per person.

Save-A-Tot
317 East 34th Street
725-7477

Save-A-Tot offers instruction in infant CPR and infant and child CPR. Classes at various locations are taught individually or in small groups. The fee is $60 per person or $100 per couple.

Tot-Saver
5 East 98th Street
241-8195

Conducted at Mount Sinai Hospital, these classes teach CPR techniques for infants and children as well as safety and injury prevention. The fee is $50 per person or $85 per couple for this two-session course.

The Fourth Trimester
182 East 79th Street
348-6308

The Fourth Trimester is a small, new mother's support group that meets to discuss the range of issues facing new mothers, including returning to work, postpartum blues and infant development. There are day and evening groups available to accommodate any new mom's schedule.

The New Parent's Circle
Ann Profitt, M.A.
26 West 9th Street between Fifth and Sixth Avenues
938-0139

Ann Profitt runs a variety of support groups for expectant and new parents (or just moms) at two locations in Battery Park and Greenwich Village. The groups discuss adjusting to the new role of parenthood, changes in the marital relationship, and work issues. Ann also does private and couples counseling and will put together workshops or seminars for the community.

The Parent Child Center
247 East 82nd Street
879-6900

The Parent Child Center, affiliated with the New York Psychoanalytical Society, offers weekly play and discussion groups on

Monday and Wednesday mornings for parents of babies and toddlers. While children play, parents hear about parenting and child development issues followed by a question and answer period. The cost is $480 for a sixteen-week session.

Parenting Horizons*
Central Presbyterian Church
593 Park Avenue at 64th Street
Rutgers Presbyterian Church
236 West 73rd Street 765-2377

Julie Ross teaches "Active Parenting," which covers how to handle tantrums, how to help children sleep at night, learn to brush their teeth, get dressed for school, and perform other daily tasks. Julie works to build parental confidence and gives practical examples of what to do when a particular situation arises. Classes meet weekly for nine weeks. This is an excellent class for parents of toddlers.

The Soho Parenting Center
568 Broadway, Suite 205
334-3744

The Parenting Center, a respected downtown resource for new moms, organizes vari-

ous mother/infant support groups during the day and in the evenings. The center offers a second-time mother's group and both private and group parent counseling sessions.

Elizabeth Bing Center for Parents
164 West 79th Street
362-5304

The Elizabeth Bing Center conducts several classes for new moms and dads, including seminars on parenting, baby safety, and breastfeeding. Each seminar is approximately one and one-half hours and costs $50. The center also offers a Lamaze refresher class for second-time parents.

The Early Childhood Development Center
163 East 93rd Street
360-7803

The center conducts weekly meetings to discuss sleeping, feeding, crying, and other early child-raising issues.

Educational Alliance Parenting and Family Center at the Sol Goldman YM-YWHA*, 344 East 14th Street
780-0800 ext. 239

The Educational Alliance, a nonprofit

organization, is a great New York City resource, with a variety of wonderful workshops for parents and classes for children of all ages. For new moms, the alliance offers New Parents Stroll In, an open discussion led by the director of the Parenting and Family Center, Kiki Schaffer. The group meets on Tuesdays (newborn to six months), and Wednesdays (six months to one year). Each session is $12 for nonmembers, $8 for members. The Alliance also offers a workshop entitled Preparing Your Marriage for Parenthood. (Ms. Schaffer, a CSW, is available for private counseling sessions as well. She can be reached at 529-9247.) Kiki Schaffer is a real pro, and we only wish we lived closer to the Sol Goldman Y.

F. E.M.A.L.E.
Sarah Schiff
688-3750

Formerly Employed Mothers at the Leading Edge (F. E.M.A.L.E.) a non-profit organization, meets twice a month in the evenings to discuss child/home/work issues. This support group for moms who have left the workforce also helps set up playgroups. Membership is $25 for a year and includes

a newsletter from the national organization. There are East Side and West Side groups.

The Greenwich Village Center
219 Sullivan Street
254-3074

The Greenwich Village Center, part of the Children's Aid Society, has many classes for parents of newborns to teens. The center offers infant CPR and First Aid classes for parents and caregivers, and infant massage for babies age six weeks to five months; a five-session class is $75.

92nd Street Y "New Parents' Get Together"*
92nd Street YM-YWHA 1395 Lexington Ave.
996-1100

New Parents' Get Together seminars feature speakers who discuss nutrition, sleep, babies, and your marriage. (Free for members of the Y's Parenting Center, $7 for nonmembers; annual membership is $150.) There is a New Parents' Get Together on Sunday mornings for moms and dads who can't make it during the week. Other classes for new moms include postpartum exercise, caring for a newborn, and a breastfeeding workshop. The Y offers baby-sitting for children three months to four years; $7/hour for non-members and $6/hour for members.

The Rhinelander Children's Center
350 East 88th Street
876-0500

The Rhinelander Center, like the Greenwich Village Center, is part of the Children's Aid Society. For new moms and their babies, classes include infant CPR and First Aid, infant massage, and Your Baby's First Year, a three-session workshop ($60) that focuses on establishing sleeping and eating patterns, recognizing stages of development, and organizing your day. For parents of older children, there are daytime and evening discussion groups, such as Tired of Nagging and Yelling?, How to Teach Right from Wrong, and more.

New Mother's Luncheons: East Side
Ronni Soled*
744-3194

Ronni Soled, a mother and former teacher, holds a weekly luncheon series, usually on Tuesdays from 11:30 A.M. to 2:30 P.M. at an Upper East Side restaurant, for mothers and babies ages newborn to nine months .

The sessions include a little playtime, lunch, and a guest speaker, who might be a baby-proofing expert addressing home-safety issues, a pediatrician discussing eating schedules and sleeping patterns, or a pediatric dentist talking about teething and pacifiers. Lunches cost $22 each, or you can purchase a series of 5 for $95. Ronni recently launched an evening series (great for working moms) and Sunday brunches for families and dads. Ronni is an invaluable New York resource and often serves as a matchmaker for moms with babies the same age who live near each other.

New Mother's Luncheons: West Side
Lori Robinson*
769-3846

Lori Robinson, former director of special events for United Jewish Appeal, organizes lunches and events at a different restaurant each Thursday from 12 P.M. to 2 P.M. Lori's lunches are fun and informative; each one costs about $20 and attracts twenty to twenty-five moms with babies (newborn to nine months). She holds separate luncheons for moms of toddlers, and organizes evening events for working moms. Past speakers have addressed the group on making your own baby food, taking better baby pictures, and having a second baby.

The Parent's League*
115 East 82nd Street
737-7385

The Parent's League, a nonprofit organization founded thirty years ago, is a vital resource for New York parents. For a $40 annual fee, you'll have access to lectures, literature, and counseling services, plus a calendar and guide to citywide events and programs for children, a birthday party reference guide, a list of emergency telephone numbers, a newsletter, and information on schools and after-school activities. The league maintains an advisory service for schools and camps, as well as a listing of nannies, mother's helpers, and baby-sitters. You'll also receive the Parent's League Toddler Book, which contains information on classes you can take with a toddler. The Parent's League publishes and sells a guidebook to private schools that briefly describes all of the ISAAGNY (Independent Schools Admissions Association of Greater New York) member schools.

Arlene Eisenberg
"What To Expect The First Year" weekly lecture
Ansche Chesed
251 West 100th Street
865-0600

Arlene Eisenberg, one of the trio of authors who wrote the best-selling book, *What to Expect the First Year,* lectures on parenting topics. The talks are for new mothers, cost $3 each, and are offered every Wednesday at 1:30 P.M.

Elizabeth Silk, CSW
500 West End Avenue
873-6435

Elizabeth Silk, a specialist and counselor in postpartum depression and fertility issues, runs a new mother's group that meets every other week for one and one-half hours. The members of the group exchange experiences and information.

Mary Clements, R.N.
21 West 87th Street
595-4797

Mary Clements, R.N., is a breastfeeding expert and lactation consultant. (A lactation consultant teaches women how to breastfeed correctly.) She gives breastfeeding classes at Roosevelt and Lenox Hill hospitals and a course to midwives at Columbia Presbyterian Hospital. She also sponsors luncheons, held in Park Slope, Brooklyn, every two weeks, at which she speaks about breastfeeding and other new mother issues.

Sandra Jamrog
866-8257

A mother of four, Sandra Jamrog has been teaching pre- and postnatal classes for more than fifteen years and is certified by the Metropolitan New York Childbirth Education Association (718-369-0975). She offers parenting education classes for men and women and teaches postpartum exercise and relaxation techniques.

Nancy Samalin, R.N.
787-8883

Nancy Samalin runs parent guidance workshops for new and expectant parents on the Upper West Side. This three-time author lectures frequently on parenting issues.

HOTLINES, WARMLINES, AND OTHER SPECIAL HELP

There may be times during your baby's first few weeks or months when you need more specialized help or support than your pediatrician, mother, or friend can provide.

During these weeks it is a good idea to keep handy the telephone number of the nursery of the hospital in which you delivered. Often, the nurses can easily answer your questions and help you through a minor crisis. Some hospitals also have special telephone numbers set up to assist new moms. Inquire about your hospital's policy for new mother call-ins. Following are a variety of additional support groups and referral programs, as well as some important numbers to have in case of an emergency.

Adoption
Adoptive Parents Support Group
475-0222

A support group for adoptive parents.

Adoptive Parents Committee
304-8479

An adoptive parents support group with chapters in New York, Long Island, and Westchester.

At-Home Moms

American Mothers at Home
800-223-9260

A nationwide organization for stay-at-home moms. The membership fee of $25 includes a bi-monthly magazine and a resource guide that puts you in touch with support groups in your area.

Breastfeeding

La Leche League
794-4687

A worldwide volunteer organization founded by a group of mothers to support other moms who chose to breastfeed their babies. La Leche's services are free, nonsectarian, and supported by membership fees ($30 per year).

La Leche has group leaders in various parts of New York who run monthly meetings to discuss breastfeeding. They also provide a valuable telephone help service. When you call, a recording gives you the name and number of a woman who can be reached that day. A friend of Pamela's found La Leche to be a lifesaver when she couldn't figure out how to work her new electric breast pump. A La Leche volunteer spent twenty minutes on the phone with her, talking her through it.

Beth Israel Medical Center Lactation Program
420-2939

A warmline to answer breastfeeding questions and provide support for nursing mothers.

Mothers Network
875 Avenue of the Americas, Suite 2001
New York, NY 10001
239-0510

A membership organization that gives new mothers the opportunity to network with other new moms. They offer workshops, phone support, tips on childcare, shopping trips, activities, and more.

The National Association of Mothers Centers
336 Fulton Avenue Hempstead, NY 11550
516-486-6614

A referral service for mothers' groups in your area.

Hotline Help

Child Abuse and Maltreatment
Reporting Center
(800) 342-3720

A hotline to report cases of suspected child abuse.

Emergency Children's Service
966-8000

Emergency assistance for abused, assaulted, maltreated, or neglected children.

New York Foundling Hospital Crisis Intervention Nursery
472-8555

An emergency placement for a preschool child whose parent is under stress. This free service provides a cooling-off period for parents for as long as two days.

Poison Hotline
340-4494/764-7667

A service that offers immediate advice and direction in cases of poison ingestion.

Premature Infants

The best place to get advice and counseling or to find out about support groups for parents of premature babies is through your hospital's Intensive Care Nursery. Many ICNs automatically provide such support. If yours does not, ask the staff to direct you to a group in your area.

National SIDS Resource Center
800-221-SIDS (800-221-7437)

This center provides SIDS information to parents.

Single Parents

Parents Without Partners
800-637-7974

A self-help group that provides support and information about single parenting issues.

Single Mothers By Choice
988-0993

A support group for women who have had a baby on their own, without a husband or partner.

Single Parent Resource Center
947-0021

A clearinghouse of information on single parent programs in the United States and abroad.

Single Parents Support Group

780-0800 ext. 239

This group currently meets at the Educational Alliance on Monday nights from 6:15 P.M. to 7:45 P.M. Baby-sitting available by advance reservation.

Twins or More

M.O.S.T. (Mothers Of Super Twins)

516-434-6678

A support group for parents of triplets, quadruplets, or quintuplets.

National Organization of Mothers of Twins Clubs, Inc.

505-275-0955

This club provides information on local twin, triplet, and quadruplet (and more) support groups.

Special Needs Groups

The Lighthouse/New York Association for the Blind

821-9200

The Lighthouse works with blind children throughout the city and provides comprehensive services and resources for them and their families.

Cerebral Palsy

United Cerebral Palsy of New York City

677-7400

This organization offers comprehensive services for children and their families, beginning at infancy.

Cystic Fibrosis Foundation

986-8783

A foundation that provides advice, counseling, and hospital referrals for families of children with Cystic Fibrosis.

Down Syndrome Support Group

691-8097

A support group for parents of Down's syndrome babies and children.

National Down Syndrome Society

460-9330

This society offers general information, parent support, and assistance with identifying programs at local hospitals for Down syndrome babies and children.

League for the Hard of Hearing

462-4008/741-7650

Provides information on speech and hearing programs and clinics.

Pregnancy and Infant Loss Center (Bereavement Group)
612-473-9372

This center provides information on local support groups for women or couples recovering from a miscarriage or the loss of an infant.

Educational Alliance
780-0800

Educational Alliance runs workshops to help parents through pregnancy loss.

Resources for Children with Special Needs
677-4650

An information, referral, advocacy, and support center for parents of children with special needs.

Spina Bifida Information and Referral
800-621-3141

IMPORTANT SUPPLIES
Diaper Services

In our environmentally conscious age, the use of cloth diapers instead of disposables is gaining popularity. Below is a list of diaper services that deliver in the New York City area. Most offer identical services, with little variation in price. Diaper pails can be purchased from all these companies for about $10.

Nature Baby Diaper Service
48 Harold Street
Tenafly, NJ 07670
800-344-3427

Eighty newborn diapers are delivered to your house once a week (the day of week depends on where you live), and the soiled ones are picked up. The price is $15.75/week.

Rainbow Diaper Service
21C Railroad Avenue
Valley Stream, NY 11580
800-924-9697

Eighty newborn diapers are delivered to your house once a week (the day of week depends on where you live), and the soiled ones are picked up. The price is $14.95/week.

Special Deliveries Diaper Service
47 Purdy Avenue
Port Chester, NY 10573
800-582-7638 or 914-937-9184

Eighty newborn diapers are delivered to your house once a week, and the soiled ones are picked up. The price is $15.95/week. This company also produces a monthly newsletter containing helpful information on baby items available through Special Deliveries affiliates.

Diapers Direct 800-515-3427, is a new delivery service featuring Tender Touch disposables. Diapers Direct is a wholesaler, and sells at a deep discount. Newborn diapers are delivered in cases of 288 for $49.

Breast Pumps

For breastfeeding working moms or other women who would like their husbands or caregivers to feed Baby an occasional bottle of breast milk, an electric breast pump is a wonderful convenience. Electric pumps are faster and easier to use than manual or battery-operated pumps. If you plan to breastfeed for three months or less, we recommend renting an electric, hospital-grade pump. Pumps can be rented by the day, week, or month. They can also be purchased through The Right Start Catalog. Buying is a good idea if you plan to breastfeed for an extended time or if you are planning to have more children. The Medela Lactina is a good one to rent or purchase. For the nearest outlet, call Medela at: 800-TELL-YOU. The La Leche League, 794-4687, can also tell you where to rent a breast pump.

Prices for pump rental range from $50 to $70 per month. Most places sell an accompanying kit that contains sanitary accessories to be used with the pump. The kit is priced at about $30 for the single pump and $40 for the double. The single pump allows you to pump milk from one breast, and the double from both breasts at the same time.

Breast pumps can be rented at the following locations:

UPPER EAST SIDE
Booming Babies
Delivery Service
722-8722

Calagor Pharmacy
1226 Lexington Avenue at 83rd Street
369-6000

Clayton & Edwards Pharmacy
1327 York Avenue at 71st Street
737-6240

Falk Drug
259 East 72nd Street
744-8080

Kings Lexington Pharmacy
1091 Lexington Avenue at 77th Street
794-7100

McKay Drugs
1296 Third Avenue at 74th Street
794-7000

Timmerman Pharmacy*
799 Lexington Avenue at 61st Street
838-6450

UPPER WEST SIDE
Albee's
715 Amsterdam Avenue at 95th Street
662-8902

Apthorp Pharmacy*
2201 Broadway at 78th Street
877-3480

Brant Chemists*
267-A Amsterdam Avenue at 72nd Street
362-5480

Chateau Drug
181 Amsterdam Avenue at 69th Street
877-6390

Regine Kids
2688 Broadway at 103rd Street 864-8705

Suba Pharmacy
2721 Broadway at 104th Street
866-6700

Westerly Pharmacy
911 Eighth Avenue at 54th Street
247-1096

DOWNTOWN
Barren Hospital Medical Center
49 Delancey Street at Eldridge Street
226-6164

Elm Drugs
298 First Avenue at 17th Street
777-0740

Halpern Drug & Surgical
420 Second Avenue at 24th Street
683-0148

Little Folks
123 East 23rd Street
982-9669

Miriam Goodman
Home Delivery
219-1080

5 · entertainment for kids and moms

You're through the first couple of months; you're getting a handle on this motherhood business; you have packing the diaper bag down to a science. You're ready to venture out with your little one and start having some fun!

You and your baby can roll around on a mat together at the 92nd Street Y, get some culture at the Temple of Dendur at the Met, relax at an outdoor café, or stroll to a neighborhood playground and meet other moms and their little ones.

In this chapter, we'll give you a rundown of the Mommy and Me classes and activities available in the city. (Unless otherwise indicated, caregivers, dads, or grandmas are also welcome to take their young charges to these classes.) Then we'll turn to New York's playgrounds and parks, museums, indoor play spaces, child-friendly restaurants, and other special spaces where you and your baby can have a good time.

MOMMY AND ME CLASSES AND PROGRAMS

As your child grows, she is going to learn to run, jump, tumble, sing songs, and scribble pictures all on her own—she doesn't need to attend a class to learn them. But classes can help her develop social skills, learn how to function in groups, be disciplined, and acquire a host of other skills. Above all, children seem to enjoy themselves in these programs, and it's nice to have some places to go during New York winters.

All these places and programs offer classes for children age three and under. Some take babies as young as three months. However, you and your child will find an organized class much more enjoyable if she is able to sit up on her own, so it's a good idea to wait until your baby is at least six to nine months old before signing up.

Here are some guidelines to follow as you check out these programs:

Take a trial class or attend an open house before you sign up. You may have to pay for it, but you'll have a better sense of what you are getting into.

✳ Look for classes with children the same age as your own.

✳ Look for big, open, clean rooms with plenty of space and light, accessible by elevator or ramp. You should not have to walk up five flights of stairs carrying your baby, diaper bag, and stroller.

✳ Equipment should be scaled down to small-child size, and any gymnastic-type facilities should include lots of mats and other safety features.

✳ Small to medium size classes are best. Do not be too concerned if a class is very big on the first day, because everyone is not there every week. Illness, naps, and vacations normally account for a quarter of a class being absent in any given week.

✳ The teacher makes all the difference—some are better than others. The other children and their mothers and nannies also can affect the atmosphere of a class. If you are the only mom in attendance, for example, you may feel awkward spending time with ten nannies every Thursday afternoon at two o'clock.

✳ Location is important. Enroll in a class near your home. If you can push your baby in the stroller, less than ten blocks, you will be more likely to attend and to make it there on time.

Prices and schedules change almost every semester, so call ahead for the latest information. Classes often run in sessions of seventeen to nineteen weeks; prices range from $250 to $350. During the summer, many places—Jodi's Gym and the 92nd Street Y, for example—offer four-, six-, and nine-week sessions that cost from $80 to $150. There are so many opportunities for you and your child, as you will see in the following section. Take advantage of one or more.

Asphalt Green Inc.

The Murphy Center
555 East 90th Street 369-8890
Age: 6 months and up

Swimming classes for young children at Asphalt Green, a fitness and sports complex, are held in the warm water Delacorte Pool (not the Olympic size pool) under excellent supervision. Water Babies is for six- to eighteen-month-olds. It accustoms them to being in the water through soothing games and songs. Water Tots, for children eighteen to thirty-six months, teaches kicking, arm movements, and prone floating. The curriculum incorporates the teaching methods of both the American Red Cross and the American Swim Coaches Association. Adults must go in the water with children under four.

Buckle My Shoe

40 Worth Street at Church Street
374-1489
Age: 3 months to 5 years

Mommy and baby classes at this day care center focus on creative play and movement.

CATS (Children's Athletic Training School)*

Rutgers Presbyterian Church
236 West 73rd Street 877-3154
Central Presbyterian Church 539 Park Avenue
at 64th Street 751-4876
Age: 1 year and up

CATS is the only comprehensive children's sports training program for one- to ten- year-olds in the United States. Baby CATS and Kiddie CATS meet once a week in a large auditoriumlike space; children under two years play on gym equipment such as slides and tunnels. Classes are large, at least twenty toddlers with moms or caregivers, but there are three coaches for each session. Many children stay with the program for years, going on to take lessons in tennis, soccer, golf, hockey, or basketball.

Chelsea Piers

Pier 62, 23rd Street and 12th Avenue
336-6500

Age: 15 months and up

In addition to their extensive adult offerings, Chelsea Piers, the largest sports complex
in New York, offers programs and facilities for
very young children. Pier Play, for ages fifteen
months to three years, uses directed play such
as games, art, and drama to encourage children to share, ask questions, and otherwise get
involved in the class. For physical activity, enroll
your child in the preschool gymnastics program
(seventeen months to five years), or take her to
the Toddler gym, where she can crawl, roll, and
jump on mats and equipment designed to help
develop basic skills. Two hours at the Toddler
Gym is $6; call for other prices.

Child's Play

Central Presbyterian Church
593 Park Avenue at 64th Street 838-1504
Rutgers Presbyterian Church
236 West 73rd Street 838-1504
Age: 6 months to 5 years

Child's Play offers a combination of free
play, games, singing, and art projects for
parents and children (no caregivers).
Babyplay is for children four to twelve months
old; Playgroup, the toddler class, is for children twelve to thirty months old.

Children's Tumbling

Sue Ellen Epstein
9-15 Murray Street at City Hall
233-3418
Age: 18 months to 10 years

Downtown moms think highly of this
tumbling and gymnastic program for children
over eighteen months. Classes are a special
combination of dance, gymnastics, and
theater. The culmination of each semester
is a show, with dramatic lighting and music,
in which the children showcase what they've
learned. Classes for toddlers are kept small
(six or seven children), last an hour, and
meet once a week.

Church Street School for Music and Art

74 Warren Street at West Broadway
571-7290
Age: 2 years and up

This proven program teaches music,
movement, art, and instruments. Toddler
classes (for two-and three-year-olds) run forty
minutes with ten children, a teacher, instructor, and mommies or caregivers. Church
Street School features the Dalcroze method
of music instruction, which combines music
awareness and movement.

Circus Gymnastics

2121 Broadway at 74th Street 799-3755

Age: 6 months and up

Mommy & Me is a forty-minute class that includes free play on gymnastic equipment, a parachute, a ball pit, a moonwalk, and circle games. The classes are for children from six months to three years. Some instructors are particularly skilled in working with young children; and you and your little one can have a great time.

Columbus Gym*

606 Columbus Avenue at 89th Street
2nd floor 721-0090

Age: 12 months and up

The facilities at Columbus Gym are some of the nicest and newest in the city: there are tunnels, trampolines, balance beams, and hills to climb over and through. Gymnastic classes for toddlers twelve to eighteen months are with mom or caregiver. For older toddlers, there's PEP (Preschool Enrichment Program), a ninety-minute minipreschool class including gym, arts and crafts, music, and storytime. Pamela and Rebecca took the PEP class for a year and enjoyed it tremendously.

Diller-Quaile School Of Music

24 East 94th Street 369-1484

Age: 1 year and up

Diller-Quaile is a New York institution. There are music classes for toddlers and moms, as well as private instruction on different instruments. Classes begin in September and run until May. Music Babies, for those aged twelve to fifteen months, teaches lullabies, finger plays, nursery chants, and a variety of playful rhythmic activities. Music for Nearly Twos uses movement activities, games, and percussion instruments to guide classroom play. There are ten to twelve children in a class, with three instructors for children under eighteen months. Note: The application process begins one year in advance of classes. Call for more information. Classes start at $1,000 for about thirty sessions.

Discovery Programs

424 East 89th Street
251 West 100th Street 749-8717

Age: 3 months to 12 years

Gym for Tots takes place in a gymnastic playroom where children are encouraged to run, jump, climb, balance, bounce, roll, and swing, with a parent or caregiver. Music,

Dance and Storytime is a program of movement games, action songs, finger play, and friendship. In the toddler art classes, children use brushes, finger paints, sponges, and other materials to explore the world of shape, color, and texture.

The Early Ear
48 West 68th Street 877-7125
Age: 6 months to 3 years

The Early Ear is a highly-regarded introduction to music for babies as young as six months. Each class has ten children, with one teacher and two accompanists, one on piano and the other on violin. Classes are forty minutes and incorporate sing-a-long, games, and play activities. The cost of each fifteen-week session is $245.

Educational Alliance Parenting and Family Center at The Sol Goldman YMHA*
344 East 14th Street 780-0800 ext. 239
Age: newborn to 36 months

The Educational Alliance Parenting Center offers Mommy and Me and Two x Two play classes that concentrate on play, music, and song, as well as a variety of multi-cultural classes. Classes last from forty-five minutes to two hours and are limited to twelve children and adults. They also have a monthly Me and My Dad group, a three-session workshop for new parents called From Pair to Parent, evening groups for working and single parents, and other parenting classes. You can join the new 14th Street Y for a yearly fee which entitles you to program discounts, special events, priority registration, and pool and gym facilities. Classes have member and non-member fees. Kiki Schaffer, the director, creates a special sense of community and is an encyclopedic resource for the downtown parent.

Elliott's Gym and Studio For the Arts, Inc.*
65 West 70th Street at Columbus Avenue
595-0260
Age: 10 months to adult

Elliott's offers a variety of Mommy and Me classes including tumbling, music and movement, and gymnastics. Classes for infants focus on jumping, climbing, pushing, pulling, rolling, and free play. Art classes for toddlers (eighteen to thirty-six months) encourage children to use all five senses to explore shapes and textures and use recycled and found objects. There's also a special class for twins. Elliott teaches many classes himself and is terrific with kids. Note: Elliott's offers a free half hour class for families of children newborn to ten months.

Funworks for Kids
225 East 51st Street
112 East 75th Street 759-1937
Age: 9 months to 3 years

Funworks offers a ninety-minute class—a preschool-type program—featuring free play, circle-time singing, dance and gym activities with balls, parachutes, and air mattress, plus an art project and storytime. This program has a loyal following and moms praise the extended program, especially for toddlers, as well as the variety of activities offered in each class.

Gymboree
401 East 84th Street
50 Lexington Avenue at 24th Street
30 West 68th Street
210 West 91 Street
64 West 3rd Street 308-6353
Age: 3 months to 4 years

These popular, organized play groups are the original baby classes. Gymboree features circle games and songs, free play on gymnastic-style equipment, exercise games, and parachute play. There are about twelve children to one teacher in each class. Classes meet once a week for forty-five minutes. Join Gymboree at any time, and they will pro-rate their fees. Check out the location you're interested in; facilities vary somewhat.

Gymtime
1520 York Avenue at 80th Street
861-7732
Age: 5 months to 14 years

Gymtime offers organized play groups that feature songs, games, and circle time for mother and child in clean, brightly lit rooms with gymnastic-style equipment. You'll also find a variety of classes, including cooking and art for toddlers. There can be up to fifteen children in a class with two instructors; classes meet once a week for forty-five minutes. Gymtime will pro-rate their prices for any latecomers.

Jodi's Gym*
244 East 84th Street 772-7633
Age: 6 months to 12 years

Classes in this brightly colored, well-padded facility feature free play time, singing, stretching, and an obstacle course. Jodi is always around, and personally trains all her instructors, who are certified by the USA Gymnastic Federation. Classes for children under two have slides, ladders, tunnels, balls, and parachutes that are just right for tiny hands and feet. Classes are forty minutes, and there is a maximum of sixteen children to a class with two instructors. Jodi's Gym has wonderful minisummer camp sessions for children two and one-half years and up, with gym, art, music, snack, and storytime three days a week for two hours a day.

Judy Stevens Playgroup*

77 Franklin Street at Church Street

941-0542

Age: 2 to 3 years

Judy Stevens, an artist and a mother, started forming play groups for downtown moms thirteen years ago. What special play groups! There are only six toddlers in a class. Judy does art projects and activities with lots of music, movement, and free play in a warm, child-friendly loft. Classes meet either two or three times a week from 9:30 A.M. to 1:30 P.M. and lunch is served. There is always a waiting list.

Just for Tots

888 Lexington Avenue at 65th Street

396-0830

Age: 12 months to 5 years

In 1973, François Thibaut created the Language Workshops for small children, which are still popular today. Thibaut and his colleagues opened Just for Tots in March 1995 where you'll find a variety of forty-five-minute programs for toddlers, including arts and crafts, music and movement, and gymnastics in addition to the language classes.

Kids Co-Motion

579 Broadway at Prince Street

West Park Presbyterian Church

165 West 86th Street 431-8489

Age: 12 months and up

This creative movement program has classes that feature light tumbling, ballet, and music for children as young as one year. Rebecca Kelly, the founder and teacher, runs the two locations with her husband and emphasizes a joyful, positive learning experience. Classes run for fifteen weeks.

Kindermusik

Zion-St. Mark's Lutheran Church

339 East 84th Street

120 West 76th Street 864-2476

Age: 18 months to 3 years

Kindermusik is an international movement with more than 2,100 teachers. This introductory music class gets toddlers singing, chanting, dancing, and playing simple instruments like rhythm sticks, bells, and drums. Now that Kindermusik is part of the Gymboree company, classes are taught at their locations in addition to those listed above. The sessions are forty-five minutes long, and children can participate with either a parent or caregiver.

Life Sport Gymnastics

West Park Presbyterian Church

165 West 86th Street 769-3131

Age: 2 years and up

Rudy Van Daele has been teaching gymnastics for fifteen years. Classes here are small, with seven to eight students, and include activities on mats, trampolines, beams, and horses. Children are encouraged to try whatever interests them, from cartwheels to flips and more.

Lucy Moses School, a division of the Elaine Kaufman Cultural Center

Abraham Goodman House

129 West 67th Street   362-8060

Age: 18 months and up

In Music Mates, toddlers sing, dance, and learn about different instruments with beloved teachers Abe and Mickie Mandel. The school offers a class that combines rhythm games, creative movement, and dramatic play; and there's a number of music, movement, and dance classes for older preschoolers. Children attend with parents or caregivers.

Mary Ann Hall's Music for Children*

The Church of Heavenly Rest

2 East 90th Street

203-454-7484/800-633-0078

Age: 12 months and up

Mary Ann plays the piano as children walk, march, gallop, and run to the appropriate accompaniment. She leads the group in various songs and free play with a variety of musical instruments. Classes, of not more than ten children each, run from October to May, meeting once a week for forty minutes. This is one of Kelly and Alexander's favorites.

Mommy and Me

The Greenwich Village Center
(a.k.a. The Children's Aid Society)
219 Sullivan Street at West 3rd Street
254-3074
Age: 9 months to 1 1/2 years

Children play with toys, sing songs, and listen to stories. The Greenwich Village Center, which opened in September 1993, has a variety of classes for children up to prekindergarten, as well as art classes in the afternoons for primary school children. There are usually eight to ten children in a class with one teacher.

Music Together

102 West 75th Street 473-9594
240 West 98th Street, Suite 1E 473-9594
48 East 80th Street 244-3046
Age: 6 months to 4 years

Music Together is a forty-five minute class for mommies and children in which they sing, dance, chant, and play with various instruments. At the beginning of the program, parents receive a cassette tape and sheet music. They are encouraged to play the tape at home, and moms report that their children come to know and love the songs. Music

Together has ten to twelve children per class with one instructor. Classes are not divided by age—infants and toddlers are mixed together.

Playorena

1296 Lexington Avenue at 87th Street
516-883-PLAY
Age: 3 months and up

Children bounce, crawl, climb, jump, sing, and dance in classes that are grouped by age, with about twelve children in a class with mom or caregiver and instructor. You can arrange to take a trial class for free.

Seventy-Fourth Street Magic

510 East 74th Street 737-2989
Age: 6 months and up

Seventy-Fourth Street Magic is held in a clean, bright, and large play space made up of two gyms. The gym for children over one year has padded tunnels, bridges, and houses, while the baby gym, for children under a year, is filled with a bubble pen and big balls. Classes focus on music, art, and gymnastics, and run from forty-five minutes to an hour. They usually have ten children with two instructors. They also offer cooking, drama, and science activities.

Sokol New York Gym

420 East 71st Street 861-8206

Age: 10 months and up

Sokol offers Mommy and Me classes for infants, and a toddler gym class for two- and three-year-olds. Classes consist of free play, circle time, parachute play, bubbles, and more, with a different theme every few weeks. This is one of the most reasonably priced programs in New York—$310 for a once-a-week, forty-five-minute class— and it runs from September through May.

Sutton Gym

20 Cooper Square at 5th Street
533-9390

Age: 18 months and up

Classes in this large, clean gym emphasize stretching and strengthening. The small beams, barres, and mats are perfect for toddlers. There's a tumbling track as well. The friendly and helpful staff encourages visits before signing up. Classes run for eighteen weeks and have six children per instructor.

Take Me to the Water

355 East 77th Street
717-6537/721-5433

Age: 6 months and up

Heather Silver teaches private, semiprivate, and group swimming classes. Classes at Take Me to the Water can be as small as three babies and mothers with one instructor, and are taught at various public and private pools around the city, including 74th at York, 48th at Broadway, 91st at Columbus, and in Battery Park. Classes parallel the school year; none are held in the summer. You can take as few as four classes for $150.

The Rhinelander Children's Center

350 East 88th Street 876-0500

Age: newborn to 2 years

Mommy and Me classes, early childhood development programs, and evening parenting seminars are all taught here. The Just Beginning class, for ten- to fifteen-month-olds, offers music, song, and free play for forty-five minutes. Also available at the center is Toddler Time for eighteen- to twenty-four-month-olds and thirty- to thirty-six-month-olds, and Kiddie Crafter, an art class for toddlers age two and one-half to three and one-half years. Classes usually have fifteen children to two instructors. Rhinelander is a very popular Upper East Side community center. Classes fill quickly, so apply promptly.

Tumble-Time, Inc.
Baruch College
17 Lexington Avenue at 23rd Street
Room 1125, 802-5600
Age: 6 months and up

Classes at Tumble-Time become more structured as children get older, but all have an active tone and many use padded gymnastic-style equipment with the usual music, bubbles, and songs. Until the age of three, parent participation is required; all classes are forty minutes long.

Turtle Bay Music School
244 East 52nd Street 758-8811
Age: 18 months to adult

Turtle Bay, founded in 1925, is a full-service music school that offers private music classes in all instruments. Music and movement classes start for toddlers at eighteen months, and there are programs for two-and three-year-olds as well. The Mommy and Me classes focus on movement, song, and percussion instruments. This warm and friendly school is ideal for midtown families.

YWHA 92nd Street*
1395 Lexington Avenue at 92nd Street
415-5600
Age: Newborn to adult

The 92nd Street Y's Parenting Center has a variety of activities and outstanding programs for parents and children, which make it a nationwide model. Classes include caring for a newborn, breastfeeding, baby massage, Rock 'N' Roll Baby, Little Explorers, and Parkbench. A $150 membership in the Parenting Center allows you preregistration priority in classes for three terms, special prices for every class, a free weekly lecture series on various infant and toddler child-rearing issues, and special discounts at children's stores around the city.

For West Side parents, the 92nd Street Y offers a limited number of classes at the Spanish-Portugese Synagogue at West 70th Street and Central Park West.

Each of the following Y Associations offers a variety of classes for your baby, from gymnastics to music to swimming. Call your nearest Y for information.

THE Y ASSOCIATIONS

YMCA of the City of New York

610 Lexington Avenue at 53rd Street

755-4500

Vanderbilt YMCA

224 East 47th Street 755-2410

YMCA

5 West 63rd Street 875-4139/875-4112

McBurney YMCA

215 West 23rd Street 741-9210

PLAYGROUNDS

New York's parks and playgrounds provide just about every activity you can think of. The park is a great place for your baby or toddler to explore, swing, slide, and climb, and for you to meet other moms with children close in age to yours. And when the weather's nice, you'll love going out, enjoying a change of scenery, and breathing some fresh air.

The Department of Parks and Recreation oversees some 1,578 parks and 862 playgrounds around the city. In the past few years, many playgrounds have been renovated and now have soft rubber mat surfaces, brightly colored metal bars for climbing, and sprinklers for cooling. One of the city's most original playgrounds is the Rustic Playground at East 67th Street, a perfect stop before or after a visit to the Central Park Zoo.

You can call the Parks Department at 360-8111 for information on events in any of the city's parks. For older children, call the department's recreation office at 16 West 61st Street, 408-0243, to find out about playground programs, sports, and Arts in the Park—a summer series of free activities and performances for children.

Central Park

You can easily spend a leisurely day in Central Park with your little one. Walk around the Boat Pond (68th Street at Fifth Avenue), or sit in an outdoor café and watch the miniature boat enthusiasts sail their remote-controlled beauties across the pond. Run through the Sheep Meadow (67th Street at midpark) or Strawberry Fields (72nd Street at Central Park West); bring a ball for a game of catch and some nibbles for a picnic lunch. Or buy one from a nearby concession stand.

Some of our favorite Central Park spots are: *Alice in Wonderland statue* (68th Street at Fifth Avenue). As soon as your youngster is moving around comfortably on her own, she'll be fascinated by this huge, bronze statue that's full of nooks and crannies to climb on. There are always lots of kids, with moms and caregivers sitting on the nearby benches keeping an eye on things.

James Michael Levin Playground (77th Street at Fifth Avenue). This newly renovated playground has a padded gym/slide good for eighteen-month-olds and up; space to run, play, or ride a tricycle; an enclosed swing area; a big, roomy sandbox; and a toddler-friendly water sprinkler system for hot summer days.

Spector Playground (85th Street at Central Park West). A West Side favorite, this playground has an area for children under two, with a sandbox, slides, climbing equipment, and a black-top space for tricycles and toy cars. For children over two, a sandy section of the playground has tire and rope swings, climbing chains, and more.

Adventure Playground (next to Tavern on the Green, West 67th Street at Central Park West). Divided into two sections, a lower play area has baby swings, a sandbox, slides, and a bridge, while the hilltop playground, for older kids, resembles an Egyptian park!

Diana Ross Playground (81st Street at Central Park West). This is the perfect place to go with your new baby or visiting five-year-old niece—it has baby swings as well as great climbing equipment for older kids.

You'll undoubtedly find your own favorite parts of Central Park. And, of course, you'll pay many visits to these two special attractions:

The Central Park Carousel
Middle of Central Park at 64th Street
879-0224
*Hours: Every day, weather permitting,
10:30 A.M. to 5 P.M.*

The Central Park Carousel is one of this country's great antique carousels. Each ride lasts about five minutes and is accompanied by calliope music. Your baby can ride with you on a horse that moves up and down, on a stationary horse, or in one of two chariots. Each ride costs ninety cents per person.

Central Park Wildlife Conservation Center (Zoo)
Fifth Avenue at 64th Street 861-6030
*Hours: Monday through Friday 10 A.M.
to 5 P.M.; Saturday and Sunday
10:30 A.M. to 5:30 P.M.*

Officially called the Central Park Wildlife

Conservation Center, this recently renovated zoo provides natural habitats for mostly small (with the exception of the polar bear) animals. Visit the rain forest, complete with monkeys; the penguin house; and, of course, the sea lions' circular pool with see-through sides. The daily sea lion feedings are sure to delight your youngster. You'll find plenty of places to sit, as well as a cafeteria.

There are scheduled tours and activities each day (story hours, arts and crafts, and animal feedings), so call ahead. There's also a Children's Petting Zoo, currently under renovation. Adult admission is $2.50, children three to ten years pay fifty cents, and children under three are free.

Other Parks

While Central Park is the biggest and the best, New York has many other parks where your child can have some outdoor fun. Here are some favorites, by neighborhood:

EAST SIDE (EAST RIVER)

*Carl Schurz** (East End Avenue at 84th Street). This popular Upper East Side park has something for everyone—for infants, there is a play area with swings, bridges, and slides; for toddlers, there is an enclosed sandbox with climbing and sliding jungle gyms; and for adults, there is a superb riverside promenade. A paved pavilion with a sprinkler fountain running in the summer is used for ball play and tricycles in the fall and spring.

*John Jay** (FDR Drive at 76th Street). This big, clean enclosed playground has slides and moving bridges, a good central sprinkler system, a sandbox with swings for all ages, and benches all around. From the Fourth of July to early September, a large swimming pool is open from 11 A.M. to 7 P.M., and there are free swimming lessons for children ages three and up. Sign up early; the playground and pool get busy and crowded in the summer months.

You might also check out these parks:

St. Catherine's Playground
(First Avenue at 67th Street).

Sutton Place Park
(FDR Drive at 57th Street).

MacArthur Playground
(FDR Drive at 48th Street).

WEST SIDE/RIVERSIDE PARK

Hippo Park Playground (Riverside Drive at 91st Street).* One of our favorites is Hippo Playground with its seven adult and six baby hippo statues ideal for climbing. It's extremely clean, and monitored by a parents' association as well as by the Parks Department. Picnic tables, benches, slides, a sandbox, seesaws, swings, and climbing equipment are shaded by fifty-year-old oak trees. This playground was specially designed for kids ages two to seven.

Riverside Drive at 76th Street.* Here you'll find nicely divided sections for infants and toddlers, plenty of climbing equipment, swings, and a gentle circular sprinkler system. There is a separate sandbox, a nice grassy area, and a basketball court for older children nearby. Bring your sunscreen; there isn't a lot of shade.

Other Riverside Park playgrounds are located at:

Riverside Drive at 83rd Street.

Riverside Drive at 97th Street.

Riverside Drive at 110th Street.

Riverside Drive at 123rd Street.

DOWNTOWN

*Hudson River Park Playground** (Chambers at Greenwich Street). A thriving downtown favorite, this clean, enclosed playground sits across from the esplanade of the Hudson River. All the equipment is labeled by age group, and there's a separate section for tables. There are swings, a sand table, a sliding bridge, climbing structures, sprinklers, and some of the most imaginative play equipment in the city.

*Battery Park** (Battery Park City). Located at the tip of Manhattan, this park attracts a number of tourists. While the swings and slides (across from the entrance to the Staten Island Ferry) are old and outdated, the grassy park itself has a fabulous view and is a pleasant place for picnicking.

Also for downtown parents and tots:

PS 40 (Second Avenue at East 19th Street).

Union Square Park

(Broadway at East 16th Street).

Washington Square Park

(West Fourth and MacDougal Streets).

Duane Park (East Stuyvesant High School).

Abingdon Square Park

(Bleecker and Bank Streets).

PUBLIC LIBRARIES

Children ages six months and up are good candidates for short library visits. Sit and relax while your toddler listens during story time, watches a short film with popular characters, or participates in an art and crafts project.

The New York Public Library system puts out a free booklet every month listing each branch's activities for children, but proximity to your home is the key in choosing what to do. Stop in or call and see what's going on.

Library branches with children's activities are listed below, by neighborhood.

UPPER EAST SIDE
96th Street
112 East 96th Street 289-0908

67th Street
328 East 67th Street 734-1717

Webster
1465 York Avenue 288-5049

Yorkville
222 East 79th Street 744-5824

UPPER WEST SIDE
Bloomingdale
150 West 100th Street 222-8030

Columbus
742 Tenth Avenue 586-5098

Riverside
127 Amsterdam Avenue 870-1810

St. Agnes
444 Amsterdam Avenue 877-4380

MIDTOWN
Donnell Library Center
20 West 53rd Street 621-0636

This special branch boasts the largest collection of children's and young adult books in the city. Moreover, it houses Christopher Robin's original Winnie-the-Pooh stuffed animals (Pooh, Tigger, Eeyore, Piglet, and Kanga) who live in the second floor children's room.

Epiphany
228 East 23rd Street 679-2645

Hudson Park
66 Leroy Street at 7th Ave. 243-6876

Jefferson Market
425 Avenue of the Americas 243-4334

Kips Bay
446 Third Avenue 683-2520

Muhlenberg
209 West 23rd Street 924-1585

LOWER EAST SIDE

Chatham Square
33 East Broadway 964-6598

New Amsterdam
9 Murray Street 732-8186

Ottendorfer
135 Second Avenue 674-0947

Tompkins Square
33 East 10th Street 228-4747

OTHER ACTIVITIES FOR YOU AND YOUR CHILD

Everything in this section is great and worthy of a gold star.

The Bronx Zoo
185 Street at Southern Boulevard
718-220-5100
Hours: Monday through Sunday 10 A.M. to 5 P.M.

At the Bronx Zoo, the largest in the United States, animals roam in large, natural settings. The Sky Ferry take visitors through the park—a nice rest for a tired toddler and his exhausted parent. Visit the children's area, a petting zoo where youngsters can pet and feed some smaller animals and go on rides. Admission is $6.75 for adults and $3 for children three to twelve. (Wednesdays are free for everyone.) Admission to the children's zoo is an additional $3 for adults and $1.50 for children.

The Children's Museum of Manhattan
212 West 83rd Street 721-1234
Hours: Wednesday through Sunday 10 A.M. to 5 P.M.; Closed Monday and Tuesday.

This interactive museum allows young children to explore, touch, and investigate its various exhibits. The Creative Corner is an early childhood center (for ages four and under) where children can paint, color, and play with educational toys in a specially designed kids' room. Story hours, puppet shows, and other activities are offered throughout the museum. Admission is $5 for adults and children over two; children under two are free. Strollers or carriages must be folded up and checked at the door.

The Children's Museum of the Arts
72 Spring Street at Broadway 274-0986
Hours: Tuesday through Sunday 11 A.M. to 5 P.M.; Closed Monday.

You can spend an entire afternoon at this hands-on museum, which offers exhibits as well as activities for children. You and your child can do arts and crafts, make a poster for Dad, or create a T-shirt design. Slides, climbing equipment, and a dress-up corner are also available. Two- and three-year-olds love this museum. Ages eighteen months and over: $4 per person on weekdays and $5 per person on weekends.

The American Museum of Natural History
79th Street at Central Park West 769-5100
Hours: Sunday through Thursday 10 A.M.
to 5:45 P.M.; Fridays and Saturdays
10 A.M. to 8:45 P.M.

Even when the Museum of Natural History fills with toddlers and their parents, it's so huge and full of hands-on exhibits and fascinating things to see that you'll hardly notice the crowd. Little children stare in wonder at the lifelike dioramas and those spectacular dinosaurs. Parents love bringing their children to the Whale's Lair, where little ones can run around on the huge floor under the giant blue whale. And for your convenience, there's a child-friendly cafeteria, located in the basement. Adult admission is $6, children are $3, and seniors and students are $4.

Metropolitan Museum of Art
Fifth Avenue and 82nd Street 535-7710
Hours: Tuesday through Thursday and
Sunday 9:30 A.M. to 5:15 P.M.;
Friday and Saturday 9:30 A.M. to
8:45 P.M.; Closed Monday.

There are times you just need a good place to take a sleeping baby while you stroll around by yourself or with a friend. And even when your toddler is awake, the Met does have some open spaces, such as the reflecting garden, where the little one can roam. Strollers are not allowed on Sundays, but the museum will provide you with a backpack for your child when you check your stroller. We have found that our toddlers are good for about an hour. Suggested donations are $8 for adults and $4 for students and seniors. Children under twelve are admitted free.

Barnes & Noble/Barnes & Noble Junior
Locations throughout the city.

These are more like community centers than bookstores. Introduce your children to the kids' sections, where they can listen to you read a story or lie on the floor to look at books by themselves. In addition, the stores have special scheduled readings, Gymboree story time, and bedtime stories. Schedules change weekly, so call ahead or drop by for a listing of events. Most Barnes & Noble stores are open from 9 A.M. to 11 P.M; all events are free.

INDOOR PLAY SPACES

Indoor play spaces are a child's dream: places to run, jump, and climb with lots of other kids on a variety of playthings. Our experience is that it's usually better to go early in the day when the facilities tend to be less crowded and freshly cleaned. No matter how many attendants are on duty, keep a careful eye on your child. And wash your little one's hands when you leave (kiddy colds spread like wildfire). New spaces are opening all the time, but these are our favorites.

Explorations
1535 First Avenue at 80th Street
772-7612

Explorations has a nautical theme, and a sailor-suited staff monitors all activities. The facility includes tunnels and tubes to climb over and through, as well as ball pits, cubes, slides, and a trampoline. After bouncing, have lunch in the Galley, which serves sandwiches, salads, pizza, and hot dogs. There is an adult and kiddy movie/television lounge, where children can watch a variety of movies while Mom watches her choice next door. The cost is $6 per child, free for adults, and you can stay as long as you like.

Kidmazeum
80 East End Avenue at 83rd Street
327-4800

Imagine this: pay $8 per child, then come and go as often as you like for the day. Go home for lunch and a nap, if you want, and come back for the rest of the afternoon. That's how it works at Kidmazeum. What's more, Kidmazeum is big, bright, and clean. Upstairs is an active play space where children can jump in a ball pit or climb through a tunnel. Downstairs, youngsters dress up in costumes, go shopping in a mini supermarket, or play with puzzles and computers. Adults enter free at all times; parents can enjoy play time with their child for the cost of the child's admission.

My Favorite Place
265 West 87th Street 362-5320

This play space has a well-equipped toddler playroom, called the Imagination Center, located in the basement. It includes a kitchen, a kid-sized house, costumes, and trains—sure ways to spark a child's creative impulses. In addition to a toy store, the main floor has an art studio as well as a dance studio. Classes include Mommy and Me, music, arts and crafts, dance, and more. Classes are $8 a session, less for a package; the adult accompanying the child enters free. My Favorite Place is also available for private parties.

Playspace
2473 Broadway at 92nd Street
769-2300

Playspace is a big indoor playground with tubes and tunnels to climb through, an Olympic–size sandbox, slides, a little-kid climbing wall, a tree house, ride-on toys, puppets and costumes. Children from six months to six years are welcome, and there's a separate area for babies up to three-years-old, so

they're safe from big-kid play. All children must be accompanied by an adult, although the staff monitors children's activities at all times. The cost is $5.50 per person; the second parent is free. A cafe is open until one hour before closing; no outside food is allowed in.

Rain or Shine
115 East 29th Street 532-4420

This space is designed to resemble a natural rain forest, and has separate areas for infants, toddlers, and older children. There is a dress-up space, a tree house with a slide, and a large play house complete with bedrooms, kitchen, and an open art room. Adults enter free and children are admitted for $8.95. You may be limited to two hours on very busy days; otherwise, you can play all day. Downstairs has a party space and sign-up classes, such as ballet and gym.

WonderCamp*
27 West 23rd Street 243-1111

Big and exceptionally clean, Wonder-Camp is our favorite indoor playspace. Entrances and exits are carefully monitored, giving you a real sense of security, and there are lots of staff members around to entertain and guide children in various activities throughout the day. There is a special area for children under two with a small carousel and ball pit; a larger space in back with slides and tunnels; a great arts and crafts room; and a movie room, where films run continually. Members of the talented staff lead short dance sessions, sing songs, and play the guitar. The cost is $6.50 per person for unlimited play.

PLAY GROUPS

Another great way to have fun with your child and meet other mothers is to join a mother/child play group. Typically, these informal groups meet once a week in someone's apartment, at an indoor play space or museum during the winter, or at a park or playground in the summer. Parents rotate the apartment meeting places, so no one person is committed to entertaining every week. Some play groups are structured, with a mother leading activities each week; others allow the children to play freely with various toys under gentle supervision.

If you haven't come across one of these play groups, start one of your own. Ask mothers you meet in the park, at a class, in a baby store, in the pediatrician's office, or at a new mother's luncheon whether they're interested in joining such a group. Four to six children is a good number. That may sound like a big crowd for your small apartment, but on any given day one or two children will be unable to attend because they're sick, napping, or away visiting Grandma.

CONCERTS, SHOWS, AND SPECIAL EVENTS

When your child is between two and three years old, he may be ready to enjoy one of the city's many shows, concerts, or special events that are produced especially for children. Watch for:

Performances of The Big Apple Circus (at Damrosch Park behind Lincoln Center from October through December), Sesame Street Live (at The Theater at Madison Square Garden, formerly the Paramount, in February), the Madison Square Garden Ice Shows (throughout the winter), and Barney, Baby Bop, and the gang (at Radio City Music Hall in January). Call Ticketmaster or Telecharge for ticket prices and purchases.

✳ Childrens' theater shows are offered throughout the year by The Puppet Company (741-1646), Puppetworks (718-965-6058), TADA! (627-1732), The Paper Bag Players (772-4448), and Tribeca Performing Arts Center (346-8510). Call for prices, schedules and information; some shows are for children age three and over.

✳ The Lolli Pops Concert Series introduces children to classical music and the orchestra at hour-long concerts. Produced by The Little Orchestra Society (704-2100), the concerts are wonderful for children ages three to five.

✳ The Swedish Cottage Marionette Theater produces children's classics at the theater in Central Park at West 81st Street (988-9093). Kid favorites have included Cinderella, Rumpelstiltskin, and Gulliver's Travels. Tickets are $4 for children, $5 for adults. Call ahead for reservations.

KID-FRIENDLY RESTAURANTS

Yes, it is possible to dine out with your new baby or toddler. In order for a restaurant meal to be an enjoyable experience, your needs are few but vital. They are as follows: When your child is still an infant, under one year, you want a restaurant that provides stroller or carriage space and a staff that doesn't mind babies.

When your child is a toddler, a welcoming staff is even more critical since your youngster may knock over a glass of water, rip up the sugar packs, or throw flowers on the floor.

That's where the need for kid-friendly restaurants comes in. Certainly, if you have favorite neighborhood spots with food you already love, you can always look around to see whether children are dining there and whether there is adequate space next to tables for a stroller holding a sleeping infant.

But what do you do when you're in a neighborhood you don't know? For hard-core signals of kid-friendliness, look for paper covering the tables, crayons, children's menus, booster seats, highchairs, and interesting sights such as fish tanks, rock pools, gardens, shopping areas, and the like. New York's ethnic restaurants are wonderful for children. The owners usually like kids; waiters will bring them something to eat right away; and these places can be quite flexible about menu offerings. Coffee shops are good, too, but not necessarily during a frantic lunch hour.

Though we are not food critics, we know

what we like when it comes to kid-friendly criteria. Fast service (out of the restaurant in an hour), room for strollers, adequate booster seats, and good food for both generations are all important to us. We're including our top twenty favorites (out of two zillion, you understand) for you to dine *en famille*.

One note: Sure, you can take an infant anywhere in a stroller, especially if the baby is sleeping. But check first to be sure the management is amenable and that there's room for your stroller. And before you go out, consider your child's ability to sit still and eat in a somewhat mannerly fashion. Some days it might be better to stay home and order in.

UPPER EAST SIDE

Barking Dog Luncheonette
1678 Third Avenue at 94th Street
831-1800

A cozy spot with cozy food such as meat loaf, pot roast, mashed potatoes, and all-day breakfast stuff. Comfortable decor with a dog motif.

China Fun
1239 Second Avenue at 65th Street
752-0810

246 Columbus Avenue at 71st Street
580-1516

It's big and noisy and just our style. Inexpensive generous portions that kids love. In fact, we know a couple of kids hooked on the steamed vegetable dumplings.

Hi-Life Bar and Grill
1340 First Avenue at 72nd Street 249-3600
477 Amsterdam Avenue at 83rd Street
787-7199

A bar, yes, but quite friendly to kids during the non-smoky lunch time. Reasonably priced; nice wait staff. Take advantage of the kid-appealing early bird specials every weeknight until seven. We like the burgers, and don't miss the fries.

Il Vagabondo
351 East 62nd Street bet. First
& Second Avenues 832-9221

Haven't been here for a while? Remember the bocce court? Kids love it, of course. They don't have to concentrate on eating but can look at an actual ball rolling on a floor really made of dirt . . . in a restaurant! Crowded, loud, with Italian fare everybody likes.

Peppermint Park

1225 First Avenue at 66th Street 288-5054

With specialties like ice cream sodas, milkshakes, sundaes, and Belgian waffles, what's not to like? Okay, if you insist on real food first, there are the requisite hot dogs, burgers, tuna melts, and stuff. But save room for the sweets . . . and candy for sale on the way out.

Serendipity

225 East 60th Street 838-3531

A classic. You're not a New York kid until you've had a foot-long hot dog (which you'll never finish) and a frozen hot chocolate (which your mother will finish quite easily). Lots of great stuff to look at here, from the offerings near the front door to the giant clock and cool stained glass lampshades. It's also fun to walk up and down the spiral staircase. No strollers or carriages!

Tony's Di Napoli

1606 Second Avenue at 83rd Street
861-8686

An Italian favorite for East Side families, with enormous portions served family style.

Strollers not permitted at tables, so bring a car seat. Lots of room between the tables. Families come early for best service.

UPPER WEST SIDE

Boulevard

2398 Broadway at 88th Street 874-7400

Every night is a different all-you-can-eat night (BBQ ribs or shrimp or mussels or chicken) for you, and a kid's menu for the little guys. Kid platters come with french fries in a little Chinese take-out carton. There are crayons on the table to occupy your little one while you're waiting. Noisy, lots of room between tables downstairs. Sit upstairs for a great view of Broadway.

Gabriela's

685 Amsterdam Avenue at 93rd Street
961-0574

It's big, bustling, open all the time from breakfast until dinner so you can eat at odd hours, and filled with kids of all ages. Authentic Mexican fare (downright cheap) from tacos, quesadillas, enchiladas, rice and beans for the kids, to more exotic house specialties for you. Be extra early for dinner, or you'll wait.

Josephina

1900 Broadway at 63rd Street 799-1000

If you're near Lincoln Center and if you're in the mood for healthy, organic California-style eating, this is the place. Airy; roomy; kids like it.

Louie's Westside Cafe

441 Amsterdam Avenue at 81st Street
877-1900

A comfortable neighborhood place that will prepare anything your kids want. They're happy to push tables together for bigger parties.

Main Street

446 Columbus Avenue at 81st Street
873-5025

Here's where Upper West Side families meet to eat family-style meat loaf and macaroni and cheese in a spacious setting. Each child gets a cute little complimentary English muffin pizza.

MIDTOWN EAST AND WEST

Broadway Diner

590 Lexington Avenue at 52nd Street
486-8838
1726 Broadway at 55th Street 765-0909

This upscale diner is better than most but remains easy on the pocket. The food is typical American fare, including sandwiches, salads, grilled burgers, eggs, and pancakes. If you're in a hurry, this is a good choice; you'll have no problem getting in and out in less than an hour.

Metropolitan Cafe

959 First Avenue at 52nd Street 759-5600

Large, busy, and kid-friendly, Metropolitan's main attraction is its beautiful outdoor garden. The menu reflects Indonesian, French, Chinese, but mostly American influences.

Hamburger Harry's*

145 West 45th Street 840-0566
157 Chambers Street 267-4446

Known for big burgers, Harry's is casual and friendly. The menu has chicken and eggs, too, but this is the place for a burger fan.

Ellen's Stardust Diner

1377 Sixth Avenue at 56th Street
307-7575

This '50s-style diner features milkshakes, burgers, chicken, and tuna melts, as well as some Mexican dishes and an assortment of salads. The waiters sing and entertain—the kids will enjoy it as much as you will.

CHELSEA/FLATIRON
America
9 East 18th Street
505-2110

Huge, roomy, and friendly, on weekends America sets up a kids' reading area with little tables, chairs, and books. A balloon artist wanders through the restaurant making balloon hats and animals. Lots of highchairs and good food that appeals to the whole family.

Chat 'n Chew
10 East 16th Street 243-1616

It feels like you're in a tiny town in the South in the 1950s, but, of course, you could only find a place like this in New York. Plenty to look at, from antique advertising signs to old jukeboxes. Great deep-fried dishes, if you can take it. Crowded, close tables; best for booster-seat kids.

WEST VILLAGE
Cowgirl Hall of Fame
519 Hudson Street at 10th Street 633-1133

Li'l pardners from all over come to see the Western memorabilia in this cool little shop that stocks everything from sheriff badges to squirt gun holsters to bandannas to rawhide vests. The food appeals, too, with a perfectly messy Frito pie (a bag of chips split open, topped with chili) and a baked potato dessert (vanilla ice cream rolled in powdered cocoa and topped with whipped cream "sour cream" sits on a hot fudge pond).

Arturo's Pizzeria
106 West Houston Street
at Thompson Street 677-3820

Here's a neighborhood place with a low-key atmosphere friendly to kids. The brick oven pizza, their specialty, is delicious, and the service is quick. Arturo's also serves all types of salads, pastas, and chicken dishes.

EAST VILLAGE
Miracle Grill
112 First Avenue at Sixth Street 254-2353

This comfortable and reasonably-priced restaurant serves excellent black bean soup, lamb, and pork chops. Dine in the garden, if possible—it's beautiful; a nice place to relax when you've been on the go all day.

Two Boots

37 Avenue A between at 3rd Street

505-2276

The "boots" of Italy and Louisiana kick in for great pizza with creative toppings. Great decor, lots to look at, with a great party atmosphere that's enhanced by music.

CENTRAL VILLAGE/NOHO

Noho Star

330 Lafayette Street at Bleecker Street

925-0070

A standard for some Manhattanites, this restaurant's casual and comfortable atmosphere easily accommodates kids. You'll find interesting Chinese and Thai food here, as well as kid favorites like pasta, burgers, salad, and chicken.

TRIBECA

Bubby's

120 Hudson Street at North Moore Street

219-0666

The menu at this child-friendly restaurant is standard diner fare but better, with a gourmet twist. Bubby's is best known for its delicious breakfasts; it's a popular brunch spot on weekends.

The Odeon

145 West Broadway at Thomas Street

233-0507

Popular with celebrities for years, this restaurant has gained a following among downtown families. It is a cozy spot, with great food and good people-watching. The Odeon gives out crayons, proving that kids are welcome.

SOHO

Tennessee Mountain

143 Spring Street at Wooster

431-3993

It's a BBQ joint, so messy fingers and faces are a given. Bringing your children is encouraged here—they get a chef's hat and crayons. Some of the best barbecued ribs in the city; parents will go for it, too.

WALL STREET

Pipeline

2 World Financial Center

225 Liberty Street 945-2755

A terrific spot at the World Financial Center, with the Battery Park City promenade providing great space and views. The food here is American, with plenty for kids, from pastas to salads to chicken dishes.

The Chains

New York might be unique, but we still have chain restaurants, both national and local, to which you can always go with children. Special menus, reasonable prices, and highchairs are all to be expected. Popular national chains include Pizzeria Uno and T.G.I. Friday's.

Carmine's

2450 Broadway at 90th Street 362-2200
200 West 44th Street at Broadway
221-3800

Popular, family-style southern Italian. It's bustling, fun, and noisy, but the wait can be excruciatingly long. If you go with at least six people, you can make a reservation (and you'll be able to sample more dishes).

Dallas BBQ

1265 Third Avenue at 73rd Street 772-9393
27 West 72nd Street at Columbus Avenue
873-2004
132 Second Avenue at St. Marks Place
777-5574
21 University Place at Washington Square
674-4450

Inexpensive, big portions of kid favorites from ribs to burgers to corn on the cob.

EJ's Luncheonette

1271 Third Avenue at 73rd Street 472-0600
447 Amsterdam Avenue at 81st Street
873-3444
432 Sixth Avenue at 9th Street 473-5555

Tons of families come for the children's menu featuring everything from PB&J to scrambled eggs. Breakfast is served all day long—an interesting concept. What do you call it, brinner? Lines are long for weekend brunch.

John's Pizzeria

408 East 64th Street between
First and York Avenues 935-2895
48 West 65th Street
at Columbus Avenue 721-7001
278 Bleecker Street between
Sixth and Seventh Avenues 243-1680

Some New York parents we know say these thin-crust pies from a wood-burning oven are the best in the city. They *are* good, plus the service is fast; there's pasta for kids who don't eat pizza; there's plenty of room around the tables; and it's noisy, so your child won't stand out among the loud voices of all the other children. Another plus: your child can watch the chefs prepare your pizza.

La Cocina

217 W. 85th Street between
Broadway and Amsterdam 874-0770
2608 Broadway between 98th
and 99th Streets 865-7333
762 Eighth Avenue between
46th and 47th Streets 730-1860

Moderately priced but quite generous single tacos, burritos, enchiladas, and more, including large, well-deserved Margaritas for the adults. Plenty of room around the tables. Kids get to choose a marble to take home for their collections.

Ollie's Noodle Shop & Grille

200B W. 44th Street between Broadway
and Eighth Avenue 921-5988
1991 Broadway at 67th Street 595-8181
2315 Broadway at 84th Street 362-3712
2957 Broadway at 116th Street 932-3300

Early every evening, Ollie's is filled with children who love the soups, noodles—from soft to crispy; from hot to cold—plus all the classic Hong Kong style dishes. Huge portions, moderate prices, and the fastest service a parent could ever hope to find.

Royal Canadian Pancake House

2286 Broadway at 82nd Street 873-6052
1004 Second Avenue at 53rd Street
980-4131
180 Third Avenue at 17th Street 777-9288

It's breakfast anytime with huuuuuge pancakes and waffles topped with tonnnnnnns of fruit and stuff. Kids love it, but be sure to share portions with them. You'll both be stuffed. Weekend brunches are mobbed.

Theme Restaurants

The West 50s now offer big blaring restaurants of all varieties and gimmicks that are sure to attract visitors. Amid the tourists, you won't find a whole lot of New York parents popping in (waiting on line is more like it) as their first choice for dining. However, you may find yourself in that neighborhood or planning a birthday party, and these places *do* come up in conversation. So here goes:

Caroline's Comedy Nation

1612 Broadway at 49th Street 265-5555

Fashion Cafe

51 Rockefeller Plaza (51st Street)
at 5th Avenue 765-3131

Hard Rock Cafe
221 West 57th Street at Broadway
489-6565

Harley Davidson Cafe
1370 Sixth Avenue 245-6000

Jekyll & Hyde
91 Seventh Avenue South 989-7701

Mickey Mantle's
42 Central Park South 688-7777

Motown Cafe
104 West 57th Street at Sixth Avenue
581-8030

Planet Hollywood
140 West 57th Street 333-7827

Coffee Bars

It's amazing that we once lived without them, now that our lives are like Seinfeld episodes filled with double iced-mocha lattes. Even more important, that hit of caffeine, administered at opportune moments during the day, does a lot for a mother who has been called into action during the wee hours. Here are two of our favorite places to swill coffee, accompanied by babies and toddlers.

DT:UT
1626 Second Avenue at 84th Street
327-1327

This coffee bar/lounge has plenty of space for strollers. The coffee, including delicious lattes and cappuccinos, is good, and the food selection is appealing. Menu items includes sandwiches (ham & cheese, tuna fish, and more), as well as gourmet offerings. Lots of quiet corners and tables with sofas and comfortable chairs make this feel like your own living room. A relaxing place for breakfast, lunch, or just a snack—the staff never rushes you.

Starbucks
For branches, call 221-0956.

Cooper's, Timothy's (especially the 72nd Street location, where the people- watching and sunshine make it a favorite), and New World (our favorite for food) are comfortable, but we find the friendliness and the ample space at Starbucks make it a good choice for a group of stroller-bound moms. You can sit for hours and chat over a coffee, if your munchkin will let you. If you're hungry, Starbucks offers a nice selection of breakfast foods all day, plus prepared sandwiches for lunch.

6 · bathrooms

Venturing out into the world with your little one, you'll often need to find a decent bathroom. Most New York moms have had frustrating times searching for a clean, comfortable place to change a diaper. So that you don't repeat the experience, here are some good bathrooms in a variety of neighborhoods. We've noted the best places for diaper changing and nursing; all bathrooms include a handicapped stall unless otherwise noted.

EAST SIDE

If you're anywhere in midtown on the East Side, you're near a number of department stores that provide comfortable, clean bathrooms. Barney's (Madison Avenue at 61st Street), Bergdorf Goodman (Fifth Avenue at 57th Street), Bloomingdale's (Third Avenue at 59th Street), Bendel's (Fifth Avenue at 60th Street), Lord & Taylor (Fifth Avenue at 39th Street), and Saks Fifth Avenue (Fifth Avenue at 50th Street) all have bathrooms with enough stalls so that there's usually not a lineup; all include diaper changing areas and/or couches or chairs nearby or in the stalls which are suitable for diaper changing or nursing.

Here are some other East Side facilities you'll want to know about:

FAO Schwarz

767 Fifth Avenue at 59th Street

644-9400

Location: second floor

At this children's mecca, the bathrooms are appropriately baby- and child-friendly. There are five stalls, a changing table separate from the stalls, a disposable diaper receptacle, and a seating area where nursing is possible.

The New York Palace Hotel*

455 Madison Avenue at 50th Street

888-0131

Location: second floor (take stairs up one flight or the elevator)

With its clean, quiet, marble bathroom, The New York Palace is one of our favorites. There are five stalls, a chair to sit in while you nurse, and a vanity that could double as a changing table, plus lots of pay telephones nearby.

The Hotel Pierre

2 East 61st Street

838-8000

Location: main floor

This marble bathroom with five stalls (no

handicapped) has a carpeted makeup area that could be a good place to nurse or change a baby, if the bathroom is not too crowded.

The Regency Hotel

540 Park Avenue at 60th Street

759-4100

Location: main floor lobby

The bathrooms here are easy to locate. There are three stalls (no handicapped), a marble vanity shelf that could be used for diaper changing, and two chairs for nursing.

Tiffany & Company*

727 Fifth Avenue at 57th Street

755-8000

Location: mezzanine

Surprisingly, this posh store has one of the best bathrooms for changing a baby. In the handicapped stall, a diaper desk folds out into a changing table. There is also a foyer area where nursing is possible.

The Waldorf Astoria

301 Park Avenue at 50th Street

355-3000

Location: main floor lobby

The bathroom here is large (eight stalls)

and comfortable with two couches and a rest area with a glass table that can be used (carefully) as a changing table.

WEST SIDE

Manhattan Mall
100 West 32nd Street
465-0050
Locations: second, fourth, sixth, and seventh floor.
The best facility is on the seventh floor. This bathroom is well equipped for nursing or changing a baby, with a special place for disposing of diapers. It also has a seating area.

The Empire Hotel
44 West 63rd Street
265-7400
Location: mezzanine
This clean marble bathroom has a marble vanity that could double as a changing table. There are also chairs for nursing and resting. The bathroom is accessible by one flight of stairs or elevator.

New York Hilton
1335 Sixth Avenue at 53rd Street
586-7000
Location: second floor on the 54th Street side of hotel
There are numerous stalls in this large bathroom, which is often crowded because of the hotel's busy convention schedule. A vanity table can be used for diaper changing.

Macy's
151 West 34th Street
695-4400
Locations: cellar, second, sixth, and seventh floors
Your best bet here is the nicely-renovated second-floor bathroom which has numerous stalls and counter space to change diapers. The bathroom on the sixth floor has chairs that can be used for nursing.

The Mayflower Hotel
15 Central Park West at 61st Street
265-0060
Location: lobby
A small, clean bathroom. A baby could be changed on top of the marble vanity.

DOWNTOWN

ABC Carpet & Home

888 Broadway at 19th Street

473-3000

Location: second and fourth floors

The bathrooms at this furniture emporium befit its style. The second floor bathroom has an antique table for changing diapers, as well as two stalls. The changing area is large and comfortable.

Bed, Bath & Beyond

620 Avenue of the Americas at 19th Street

255-3550

Location: main floor

This clean and modern bathroom has a changing area (the popular koala bear changing station) and three stalls.

South Street Seaport

(The Fulton Market) 11 Fulton Street

732-7678 (general information)

Location: mezzanine

This bathroom is a real downtown find. It has ten stalls, and is clean and well lit. There is a resting area where it is possible to nurse or change a baby.

World Financial Center

The Winter Garden

West Street and Vesey Street

945-0505

Location: main floor

Six stalls make up this well-lit and clean bathroom. There are chairs for nursing and resting.

In addition, don't forget about:

Barnes & Noble

Locations throughout the city.

All the Barnes & Noble stores have bathrooms, and the stores with a Junior section have an oversized stall with a changing station inside.

7 · the big firsts

Nothing provides more occasions to celebrate than a baby. First, you celebrate the new arrival, with announcements ranging from traditional to avant-garde, one-of-a-kind. Then, in the ensuing months, you watch with joy as your baby grows. You celebrate such landmark occasions as getting his first haircut, buying his first pair of shoes, sitting for his first professional portrait, and throwing his first birthday party.

New York is full of specialists who will help you make the most of these special moments. Shop around, compare, and ask questions.

As your baby heads into toddlerhood, you'll want to start thinking about that truly momentous first—your child's first day of school. It's hard to appreciate when you're still wondering if your little one will ever have enough hair to warrant a real haircut, but soon—around the time he is one and one-half years old—you'll begin the daunting New York rite of passage of considering preschools. We end this chapter with a few suggestions to help you along.

BIRTH ANNOUNCEMENTS

Even in this day of e-mail and fax machines, birth announcements are still the most popular way to get the word out about the new addition to your family.

There are several options available. You can purchase ready-made cards at a stationery or party store and fill in your new baby's name, weight, size, and birth date. Or you can order through a catalog, such as H & F birth announcements—800-964-4002. The price for 100 announcements is $61.95; envelopes are an additional $12.50. Most parents we know order pre-printed cards.

It's a good idea to choose your announcements a month or so in advance of your due date. Give the manufacturer about two weeks for printing. You can get your envelopes early, and address them before the little one comes. Then, after the baby is born, call the shop with all the details, such as height, weight, sex, and time and date of birth.

New York stationers have everything you could possibly want, and they will ship your selection directly to you. Below, we list the best.

Berkeley Stationers, Inc.

19 West 44th Street 719-5181

Berkeley carries a line of announcements in all price ranges— some discounted— including Crane's and Regency. Nina, the owner, will work with you to choose exactly what you need. An order of 100 cards costs about $125.

Blacker & Kooby

1204 Madison Avenue at 88th Street 369-8308

With more than sixty companies to choose from, the selection at Blacker & Kooby is outstanding. It ranges from well-known lines like Crane's and Regency to smaller creative ones like Stacy Claire Boyd. At this popular spot, an order for 100 baby announcements starts at $150.

FranMade

250 West 89th Street 799-9428

Fran Goldman is an advertising executive by day and a card designer by night. You can choose from her existing designs or have her create one just for you. Fran's cards are hand-drawn and hand-colored. Prices are $2.25-$2.50 per card, with an additional $25 charge for a new design.

Hyde Park Stationers

1070 Madison Avenue at 80th Street

861-5710

In comfortable surroundings, you can sit and look at a variety of manufacturer's lines, including Crane's, William Arthur, Chase, Regency, Indelible Ink, and Lalli. Prices for an order of 100 cards range from $40 to $400.

Jamie Ostrow

876 Madison Avenue at 71st Street

734-8890

Beautiful announcements, as well as personal stationery and invitations, all designed by Jamie Ostrow, fill this lovely store. There are many other lines to choose from, including Crane's. An order of 100 announcements starts at $170.

Kate's Paperie

561 Broadway at Prince Street 941-9816

8 West 13th Street at Fifth Avenue 633-0570

These artful downtown stores carry an excellent selection of baby announcements, featuring many unusual and hard-to-find manufacturers, such as Sweet Pea, Indelible Ink, and Blue Mug. Customers can also design their own cards and choose from dozens of papers and type styles. The announcements are then printed by letterpress. An order of 100 cards starts at $100; the cost goes up considerably if you design your own.

Little Extras

550 Amsterdam Avenue at 86th Street

721-6161

Little Extras carries many of the top lines, such as Stacy Claire Boyd, Regency, Sweet Pea, Encore, Indelible Ink, and Lalli, all discounted. Orders of 200 or less are discounted ten percent, and orders over 200 are discounted fifteen percent. An order of 100 cards costs a little over $100. This comfortable store delivers for free if you live on the Upper East or Upper West Side.

Paper Emporium

835A Second Avenue at 44th Street

697-6573

Paper Emporium has a small, quality selection including Crane's, Regency, and Carlson Craft. This store has one of the fastest turnarounds that we saw—three days on most orders. The price range for 100 cards is from $100 to $400.

Rebecca Moss, Ltd.
510 Madison Avenue at 53rd Street
832-7671

This handsome store sells some prepackaged birth announcements, but focuses on big manufacturers' books, including those of Crane's, William Arthur, Stacy Claire Boyd, and Cross Your Heart. An order of 100 announcements costs approximately $150.

Mrs. John L. Strong
699 Madison Avenue at 62nd Street
838-3848

Elegant and exquisite,this stationer is one of the few in New York that still practices the art of hand engraving. Prices start at $500 for 100 announcements and go up according to style and detail. Mrs. John L. Strong is the engraver of choice to the city's socially prominent; she is a favorite of *Martha Stewart Living*. Some of her cards are also sold at Barney's.

Tiffany & Co.
727 Fifth Avenue at 57th Street   755-8000

Tiffany & Co. has a large stationery department offering both the Tiffany brand and some Crane lines. The Tiffany cards are simple, elegant, engraved, and costly. The average price for 100 announcements is more than $500.

Venture Stationers
1156 Madison Avenue at 85th Street
288-7235

One of the most popular East Side shops for stationery and announcements, Venture carries a large selection of manufacturers, including Stacy Claire Boyd, Sweet Pea, Crane's, Lalli, and Regency. The average price for 100 announcements is $150.

Uncle Futz
408 Amsterdam Avenue at 79th Street
799-6723

You'll find a nice assortment of birth announcements, all discounted ten percent. Manufacturers include Stacy Claire Boyd, Sweet Pean, Lalli, William Arthur, Blue Mug, and Jessy. The average price for a 100-card order is about $100.

BIRTHDAY PARTIES

Many parents love extravagant birthday parties, especially their child's first one. When

The Five Best Places To Have a Two-year-Old's Party

1. **Your home, if you have room, or a common space in your apartment building.**
2. **Any place with Bobby DooWah, the children's musical entertainer (982-5909).**
3. **The Rainbow Room at the West 63rd Street Y (875-4139).**
4. **Jodi's Gym (772-7633).**
5. **Children's Museum of Manhattan (721-1234).**

your baby hits the magic age of one, the birthday party is mostly for Mom, Dad, grandparents, and friends. A cake and a few balloons will make most one-year-olds very happy, and you'll get great photos of your baby mushing up his icing.

We like the idea of having the first birthday at home, but this may not be possible if you have a big family, many friends, and a small apartment. Happily, New York is full of places that organize parties for one-year-olds. Keep this list handy for future reference—two-

and three-year-olds can have even _____ at a party place.

Most of these sites will host a ____ days a week. They offer catering services that supply everything down to the cake and party favors, though all will let you bring your own. Prices are noted, but this *is* New York, so they may change over time. Call ahead. The Parent's League at 115 East 82nd Street (737-7285) has more party information; however, you must be a member ($40 annual fee) to use their files.

Birthday Bakers PartyMakers*
195 East 76th Street 288-7112

Characters such as Mother Goose sing, dance, and play musical instruments. Children can jump on an air log, join in a parachute game and rides, or play with a variety of toys. The cost is $500 for a one-hour party; more if you want PartyMakers to come to your home.

Chelsea Piers Gymnastics
Pier 62, 23rd Street at 12th Avenue
336-6500

Little ones spend thirty minutes in a party room and an additional hour or more in the baby gym, where they can crawl, explore, play in a ball pit, and be entertained by an instructor. For $350, ten kids can play for one and one-half hours ($13 for each additional child, per hour). Catering is provided by a nearby Chock Full O' Nuts.

Child's Play

Central Presbyterian Church
593 Park Avenue at 64th Street
838-1504

For $100 for two hours, you can rent space here and have your own party. The rental includes a playroom with toys and books, a large kitchen with a small table area, two climbing slides, two long tables with twenty chairs, a tape player, and a coffee machine. The space is available all day Tuesday, Friday, Saturday, and Sunday from September to June, and on Sunday afternoons in the summer.

Seventy-Fourth Street Magic

510 East 74th Street 737-2989

Seventy-Fourth Street Magic is a big and beautiful indoor play space. It holds parties on Friday, Saturday, and Sunday. Toddlers spend one hour in the baby gym with a super-visor/teacher who helps children with the equipment, swing, and ball pit, plus thirty minutes in the party room. One and one-half hours for twelve children costs $350 ($13 for each additional child), including balloons, as well as coffee and tea for the grown-ups.

Gymtime

1520 York Avenue at 80th Street
861-7732

Partygoers can play in the padded big or minigym spaces. Kids enjoy tumbling and crawling in the gym spaces, and participating in activities involving a trampoline, a parachute, a ball pit, and bubbles. There are also circle songs. Helium balloons are provided, along with coffee and tea for adults. The space is available Friday, Saturday, and Sunday during the school year, and Monday through Thursday in the summer. The cost is $375 for twelve children ($14 for each additional child) for one and one-half hours.

Jodi's Gym

244 East 84th Street 772-7633

On the padded gym floor, birthday party kids play for forty-five minutes with an obstacle course, air mattress, balance beams, bars, mats, parachutes, and bubbles. Then they have thirty minutes for cake and ice cream. Ten children costs $375 ($13 for each additional child). Food packages are available, including cake, juice, and paper goods for $5 per person, or $7 per person for all of the above plus pizza. Jodi's is available Monday through Friday in the summer, and Monday, Friday, Saturday, and Sunday during the school year.

Party Palace

144 East 57th Street 279-1095

Birthday parties are the only business at Party Palace. Children play in the discovery area, which contains slides, video games, a moonwalk, horsey rides, and a big pool filled with balls. For $300, fifteen children can play for one hour and forty-five minutes ($15 for each additional child). Party Palace is open seven days a week, and requires several weeks' notice. You can bring your own refreshments.

Party Poopers*

104 Reade Street at Broadway 587-9030

Party Poopers creates theme parties of your choice at spaces throughout the city. A two-hour carnival-theme party, for fifteen children and twenty adults, is $999 and includes costumes, dancing, snacks, soda and juice, balloons, and paper goods. Other parties are available at different prices; some include entertainers who sing, dance, and involve the children in parades and sing-alongs. Also available is a costume closet, a tiny castle to play in, toys, a moonwalk, and face painting.

Playspace

2473 Broadway at 92nd Street
769-2300

Parties last for two hours, during which a staff member helps children explore a playground with riding toys, building blocks, a slide, a huge sandbox, xylophones, trains, basketball hoops, and a dress-up theater with costumes. After playtime, refreshments are served in a party room. The cost is $129 for ten children during the week and $169 on weekends ($11.95 for each additional child). This includes juice, coffee for adults, and a helium balloon for each child. For $199 for ten children during the week or $249 on weekends ($14.95 for each additional child), you get all of the above, plus invitation cards and envelopes, paper goods, pizza, a Carvel cake, and a Playspace T-shirt for the birthday child.

WonderCamp*

27 West 23rd Street 243-1111

WonderCamp has a carousel and a small gym/play area with slides, ball pits, and tunnels for children under two. There are live stage shows every half hour, puppet shows, singing and dancing, storytelling, arts and crafts, juggling, and a movie room. In private party cabins, an entertainer sings, performs a skit, or tells a story. A party counselor greets the children and supervises play and sing-alongs. WonderCamp has several birthday packages available, from $130 to $330 for ten children with a fee for each additional child; $5 for each adult during the week and $5.50 for each adult on the weekends. All parties last two hours and include invitations, a balloon for each child, cake, soda, or juice. The pricier packages include food and additional favors.

If you're having a party at home and want to hire entertainment, check these out:

Amazing Shawnee (costumed character and magic show), 387-7489

Bobby DooWah (music with instruments and dancing or a puppet show), 982-5909 or 772-7633 (Jodi's Gym)

Cynthia's Musical Parties (music and instruments), 717-6141

Hollywood Pop Gallery (all kinds of costumed characters), 777-2238

Madeleine the Magician 475-7785

Marcia the Magical Moose (costumed moose character and puppet show), 567-0682

Magical Musical Marion (costumed character and music), 302-1419

Only Perfect Parties (variety of themed characters and shows), 869-6988

Send in the Clowns (variety of themed characters and shows), 718-353-8446

BIRTHDAY CAKES

Everybody has a bakery in the neighborhood that makes perfectly fine, even fabulous birthday cakes. Explore your neighborhood, and be sure to ask other moms where they get cakes. Heck, you can probably get a cake from the supermarket complete with your baby's name and ubiquitous frosting flowers. But for your child's first birthday, we bet you'll want to go all out. We've listed some makers of outstanding (though sometimes outrageously priced) birthday cakes, and clued you in on which will incorporate themes such as Superman, ballerinas, or Peter Rabbit.

Cakes 'N Shapes*
245-2388

For about $100, Edie Rigberg can create a sculpture of everything from a ballerina to a teddy bear, Batman, or Superman sculpture on a cake that serves twenty-five people. A simple round cake for twenty-five costs $75. Order at least one week in advance. Pamela got a Halloween-themed cake for Rebecca's third birthday, and it was delicious.

CBK Cookies of New York*
366 Amsterdam Avenue at 77th Street
787-7702
226 East 83rd Street 794-3383

You can order chocolate or vanilla single-sheet or double-layer cakes in various styles, including cakes baked in the shape of a character of your choice.
A basic decorated cake that serves approximately twenty people costs $50. These cakes are so special, CBK makes only two a day, so order at least a month in advance. They make wonderful cupcakes, too. Delivery is extra.

Cupcake Cafe*
522 Ninth Avenue at 39th Street
465-1530

Cupcake Cafe is one of our favorites, and Kelly buys many of her cakes here. A round cake serving fifteen to twenty-five people with flowers and an inscription costs $40. A theme cake with Big Bird or Barney, serving twenty-five people, is $50. Call one day in advance to pick up a cake Monday through Saturday; call Thursday for a cake to be ready on Sunday. Delivery is $25. No credit cards; cash or check only.

Custom Made Cakes by Melissa
582-6043

Melissa Bogursky can top her cakes with 3-D sugar figures of any character, or even race cars. A cake that serves twenty-five people begins around $125. Call at least a week in advance. Delivery is free in Manhattan.

Dean & Deluca

560 Broadway at Spring Street 226-6800

Dean & Deluca's chocolate cake is phenomenal. A layer cake that serves twenty-five starts at $50. Order a day ahead—although some moms have been lucky enough to walk in and find one already made.

Grace's Market Place

1237 Third Avenue at 71st Street
737-0600

Grace's has a wide selection, including carrot and chocolate mousse cakes; some are beautifully decorated with flowers and scrolls of dark chocolate. A cake serving twelve people costs $25. You can stop by Grace's on the spur of the moment and find a cake—perhaps their delicous $16 American Beauty chocolate cake. They will customize (no kids' stuff) with three days notice. No delivery.

Kathy's Kitchen

645 Hudson Street at Gansevoort
229-1704

For a truly special birthday treat, how about an authentic gingerbread house made by Kathy Maroney? If a Big Bird cake is what you're looking for, just bring in a picture, and Kathy can replicate it on a cake. Cakes serving twenty-five cost from $45 to $60, and should be ordered three days in advance. Delivery is additional.

Lafayette Bakery

298 Bleeker Street at 7th Avenue
242-7580

Lafayette Bakery will custom make a cake with a simple design for an extra $5 to $15 over the regular price of $40 for a cake serving twenty-five. Their cakes have fruit, custard, or mousse fillings, and can be topped with whipped cream or a variety of icings.

Magnolia Bakery

401 Bleeker Street at 11th Avenue
462-2572

Specializing in old-fashioned, homemade cakes, Magnolia Bakery offers delicious yellow or chocolate half-sheet cakes. A $60 cake serves twenty-five. They won't custom make a cake, but with a day's notice, they will personalize one. No delivery.

My Most Favorite Dessert Company
120 West 45th Street
997-5032/997-5130

Well known for delicious kosher food and desserts, Dessert Company sells a two-layer round cake (chocolate or vanilla) that serves twenty-five people and costs $65 to $75. A beautifully decorated kid-themed cake is about $80. Call three to four days in advance. Delivery is $10.

Royale Kosher Bake Shop
237 West 72nd Street 874-5642

This family bake shop is a West Side landmark, and their cakes are excellent. A two-layer round cake, serving approximately twenty-five people, costs $45; a cake with decoration starts at $50. They can copy almost any design. Call a few days in advance.

Sant Ambroeus
1000 Madison Avenue at 77th Street
570-2211

Walk past this shop and you will probably see in the window a beautiful cake with marzipan designs for a child's birthday. These confections are one-of-a-kind, with airbrushed paintings on a marzipan canvas that sits atop the cake. A two-layer round cake serves between twenty and twenty-five. Decorated any way you like, it costs $162. Delivery is free in the neighborhood.

Soutine*
104 West 70th Street 496-1450

Pamela buys wonderful cakes at this tiny bake shop. A two-layer round cake serving twenty-five people costs $50, and a cake with decoration costs an additional $5 to $10. You can customize designs and flavors. Order one to two days in advance. Delivery costs $5 to $10 in Manhattan.

Sylvia Weinstock Cakes
273 Church Street at Franklin Street
925-6698

Known in New York as "the cake lady," Sylvia's creations range from castles for birthdays to fantasies for brides. Her masterpieces start at about $350 for a cake that will serve thirty-five people. Give at least three weeks notice. Delivery is included.

Veniero Pasticceria
332 East 11th Street at First Avenue
674-7264

Famous not just for fantastic cannoli, but also for light and creamy cakes for kids. Bring in a postcard-size picture of anything you want on the cake, and they'll copy it. A round cake that serves twenty-five costs $40; $20 extra for a picture. Order two days in advance. Delivery is $6 in Manhattan.

William Greenberg Desserts

434 Sixth Avenue at 10th Street
518 Third Avenue at 34th Street 686-3344
2187 Broadway at 77th Street 580-7300
1100 Madison Avenue at 82nd Street
861-1340

Another baker well known for elaborate designs and decorations, Greenberg's produces a beautiful baby carriage cake for baby showers. They even made President Clinton's 50th birthday American flag cake. A two-layer round cake serving twenty-five costs $89.95; decorated cakes run from $225 to $265. Call at least two days in advance; longer for more elaborate creations. No delivery.

HAIRCUTS

Many New York moms take their babies to their own hair salon, or attempt to give that first trim themselves. But we think you'll want to try one of these shops that specialize in children's haircutting. Little kids are notoriously bad at sitting still, and most of these places offer fun distractions like *Barney* or *Sesame Street* videos to watch, and toy cars children can sit in. You might even come away with a first haircut diploma, a lock of hair, or a balloon. Bring some toys from home, so your child won't badger you to buy one of the pricey toys that are for sale in some of these salons.

We scoured the city and talked to our friends, and are sad to report that we have not found a kids' hair salon downtown. The best moms can do is one of the three following shops that welcome kids, though there's no kid-style entertainment. They charge $10 to $14 for a child's haircut.

Astor Place Hair Designers

2 Astor Place at Broadway 475-9854

Sigfrido's Barber Shop

381 First Avenue at 21st Street
475-9513

Nick's Hair Stylists

5 Horatio Street at 12th Street
929-3917

Throughout the rest of the city, there are a number of salons designed especially to make a child's first haircut—and every one thereafter—a memorable experience.

Cozy's Cuts for Kids

1125 Madison Avenue at 84th Street

744-1716

448 Amsterdam Avenue at 81st Street

579-2600

Hours: Monday through Saturday 10 A.M. to 6 P.M.; Closed Sunday.

Cozy's Cuts is a fun hair salon with chairs fashioned to look like cars and trucks. There's a television in front of every station, and a video library. All cuts are $22 and include a diploma for the first cut, plus a balloon. You can even have the momentous occasion video-taped. Appointments are recommended.

Fun Cuts

1567 York Avenue at 83rd Street 288-0602

Hours: Monday through Friday 10 A.M. to 6 P.M.; Saturday 9:30 A.M. to 6 P.M.

Small, colorful, and charming. Each kiddy chair has its own video monitor to keep your child occupied. After first haircuts, you'll get a photograph and a lock of your baby's hair. Cuts are $20. Appointments are recommended, though walk-ins are welcome.

Michael's Children Hair Cutting Salon*

1263 Madison Avenue at 90th Street

289-9612

Hours: Monday through Sunday 9 A.M. to 5 P.M. Closed on Saturdays and Sundays during the summer.

Many of our friends had their first haircuts at Michael's. There are toy car seats, and diplomas are given for the first haircut. Cuts are $23. No appointments are taken, so avoid the busy after-school hours. This is Kelly's favorite for infants under a year old.

The Tortoise and the Hare

1470 York Avenue at 78th Street

472-3399

Hours: Tuesday through Saturday 10 A.M. to 5:30 P.M.; Closed Sunday and Monday.

Built by Broadway set designers, The Tortoise and the Hare offers lots of brightly colored diversions, including a gigantic pocket watch on the wall with people as hands. There is also a Sony Play Station, and all your favorite videos. A haircut is $20. Appointments are recommended.

SuperCuts

For branches, call 800-SUPERCUT
(800-787-3728).

Hours: Monday through Friday 9 A.M.
to 9 P.M.; Saturday 8 A.M. to 8 P.M.;
Sunday 10 A.M. to 5 P.M.

All the salons in this chain cut infants'
and toddlers' hair, and award a diploma for
the first haircut. Salons are clean and
designed to provide quick, easy-in/easy-out
service. Appointments aren't required, but, if
you wish, you can make one with your
favorite stylist.

SHOES

Buying your child's first walking shoes is an
exciting and important task. Because your one-
or two-year-old can't tell you whether the shoes
are comfortable, watch carefully as she is
being fitted. If it seems difficult to get the shoes
on and off, they are probably too small. Shoes
should generally last at least two months: if
they seem small three weeks after you bought
them, go back and have them checked.

The salesperson at the shoe store should
measure your child's foot while he is standing.
Ask about the width of your child's foot and

don't buy a shoe that narrows greatly at the
toes. Also, look for a soft, flexible sole. A soft
sole is necessary for the first year. After that,
when your child is really walking and running,
you can buy any shoe your heart desires,
except slip-on penny loafers. Your youngster
won't develop the gripping action that a slip-
on shoe requires until he is four or five.

Bebe Thompson

1216 Lexington Avenue at 82nd Street
249-4740

Hours: Monday through Saturday
10:30 A.M. to 6 P.M.; Closed Sunday.

Although primarily a clothing store,
Bebe Thompson is one of the few places
that carries the popular and durable English
brand Doc Marten for one year and up, along
with a few other simple canvas styles.

East Side Kids Inc.*

1298 Madison Avenue at 92nd Street
360-5000

Hours: Monday through Friday 9:30 A.M.
to 6 P.M.; Saturday 9 A.M. to 6 P.M.;
Closed Sunday.

East Side Kids has a wide selection
of American and European shoes for first

walkers. They also carry such popular brand name sneakers as Nike, Reebok, Keds, and Converse. Other excellent brands include Sonnet (English), Elefanten (German), and Aster (French). The salespeople are some of the best in the city. Service is on a first-come, first-serve basis, but you can call ahead and have your name put on a waiting list. Free popcorn helps pass the time if there is a wait.

Great Feet*

1241 Lexington Avenue at 84th Street
249-0551
Hours: Monday through Wednesday, Saturday 9:30 A.M. to 5:30 P.M.; Thursday and Friday 9:30 A.M. to 7:30 P.M.; Sunday 11 A.M. to 4 P.M.

This big, bright store has areas carved out for different age groups. It carries brands like Stride Rite, Nike, Reebok, LA Gear, Elefanten, and a good variety of styles. Prices are among the best around, and the manager, Gwen, knows everything about little feet.

Harry's Shoes

2299 Broadway at 83rd Street 874-2035
Hours: Monday through Wednesday, Friday, and Saturday 10 A.M. to
6:45 P.M.; Thursday 10 A.M. to 8 P.M.; Sunday 12 P.M. to 5:30 P.M.

An Upper West Side fixture, Harry's carries a wide selection of American and European brands, including Stride Rite, Elefanten, Jumping Jacks, Shoo Be Doo, Nike, Reebok, New Balance, and Enzo. This place can get very crowded, especially on the weekends and after school.

Ibiza Kidz

42 University Place at 9th Street 505-9907
Hours: Monday through Saturday 11 A.M. to 7:30 P.M.; Sunday 12:30 P.M. to 6:30 P.M.

This clothing store carries a limited selection of children's shoes. It does have Baby Botte from France and Elefanten, two excellent brands, along with a basic sneaker that comes in either black or white.

Lester's

1522 Second Avenue at 79th Street
734-9292
Hours: Monday through Friday 10 A.M. to 7 P.M.; Saturday 10 A.M. to 6 P.M.; Sunday 12 P.M. to 5 P.M.

This Manhattan branch of the Brooklyn

chain has an impressive shoe department tucked behind the clothing. Lester's is a discount store that carries a good selection of European and American brands; there's a wide variety of styles that you wouldn't expect a discounter to stock.

Little Eric*

1131 Third Avenue at 76th Street 288-8987
1118 Madison Avenue at 83rd Street
717-1513
Hours: Monday through Friday 10 A.M. to 7 P.M.; until 6 P.M. on Madison; Saturday 10 A.M. to 6 P.M.; Sunday 12 P.M. to 6 P.M.

These stores carry a wide selection of shoes for children ages six months to seven years. Brands include Nike, Keds, Converse, Jonathan B., Enzo, Baby Botte, and Elefanten, with styles from sneakers to high-end imported designer shoes. The Little Eric store brand is also excellent. This is a child-friendly store, with plenty of space plus toys to keep children busy while they are fitted.

Shoofly

465 Amsterdam Avenue at 82nd Street
580-4390
42 Hudson Street at Duane Street
406-3270
Hours: Monday through Saturday 11 A.M. to 7 P.M.; Sunday 12 P.M. to 6 P.M.

This is one of the most stylish kiddy shoe stores in the city, carrying all the high-end brands for boys and girls such as Aster's, Baby Botte, and Deoso. There's also an excellent selection of purses, hats, barrettes, and other accessories. Try to shop during the week; weekends here are quite busy.

Two Steps*

590 Columbus Avenue at 88th Street
580-3085
Hours: Monday and Thursday 10 A.M. to 6:45 P.M.; Tuesday, Wednesday, and Friday through Sunday 10 A.M. to 6 P.M.; Closed on Sunday during the summer.

Most, if not all, of the shoes here are American made; no Stride Rite, but you will find Jumping Jacks, Little Capezio, and others. The store prides itself on carrying a variety of widths, so if your little one has exceptionally wide or narrow feet, this is the best bet on the West Side.

PHOTOGRAPHS

It doesn't take long for your drawers to become stuffed with photos taken of your adorable baby by you and your relatives. But there's a reason you've left them in the drawer: When you want a picture to put in that beautiful silver frame you got as a baby gift, it's time to go to a professional. A real photographer can work in your home, the park, or her studio, and can include parents or grandparents in the shots, as well as props such as stuffed animals to antique toys, costumes, and more.

If you don't know a photographer, here are some places to start. These are fairly traditional professionals who are well-experienced in photographing children (it's an art, truly). Ask to see their portfolios, and if you don't see the kind of work you want, ask your friends for some recommendations. Also, look for photo credits in parenting magazines. There's a good chance the photographers live in New York.

A Child's Portrait

400 East 89th Street 534-3433

A basic shoot costs $250 and includes three rolls of black-and-white and two rolls of color film. Orders for print photos usually run around $500. Photos are taken at the studio at 480 Broadway (between Broome and Grand streets). You can also choose to shoot at an outside location for an additional fee of $100. They prefer to work with babies older than four months.

Barry Burns

311 West 43rd Street 713-0100

Seventy snaps of your child, plus three 8 x 10" prints, costs $300. There is an additional $30 charge to use black-and-white film. Family portraits can be made in color or black-and-white film for $400. Most work is done in the studio, but an outside location is possible for an additional fee of $50.

Creative Photoworks

20 West 22nd Street 229-1862

Photographer Helene Glansberg is friendly, relaxed, and very patient. She takes approximately thirty-six shots of your child at her studio, or she'll come to your home or another location for an additional charge. A basic shoot starts at $125 for black-and-white film and $150 for color; prints run anywhere from $6 to $25 each.

Nina Drapacz
500 East 85th Street 772-7814

Nina Drapacz specializes in hand-colored black-and-white photos. She offers various packages: a popular one is $400 for twenty-four shots—you select two 11 x 14" and three 8 x 10" prints. An additional 5 x 7" print costs $40. She does fabulous work and is extremely accommodating. Pamela's friend Marty used her twice for family photos.

Fromex
182 East 86th Street 369-4821

Yes, this camera store charges only $19.95 for a sitting of between twelve and fifteen shots. A standard package is $39.95; the superportrait package is $139.95. Fromex works only at its 86th St. studio. We both have had good results here.

Jonathan Bourne/Joshua Hendon
130 East 63rd Street
223-8396/516-484-0768

The best-known children's photographers, Bourne/Hendon will shoot either in their studio or in your home. Their black-and-white work is stunning. A $250 deposit, required at the time of your sitting, is applied to your final purchase. You pay per print; each 8 x 10" color print costs $125, each 5 x 7" print costs $100. Location shoots are an additional $200.

Karen Michele*
157 East 61st Street 355-7576

Karen Michele has been photographing infants and toddlers for more than ten years. She will design a backdrop for your photo shoot using colorful balloons, or anything else you want. Her photos can be seen in Little Eric shoe stores and in some Barnes & Nobles. There is a shooting fee of $250; a 5 x 7" print costs $125; an 8 x 10" print costs $150; duplicates are fifty percent off. You receive approximately thirty proofs from which to choose.

Manger-Weil Photography*
1556 York Avenue at 82nd Street
717-6203

Manger Weil Photography captures children's natural expressions by making sittings as much fun as possible. They will shoot in your home, at their studio, or at an outdoor location for no additional charge. Packages are around $250 for an hour. Each 8 x 10" print is $35 and 5 x 7" prints cost $15 each.

Nancy Pindrus Photography

21 West 68th Street 799-8167

Nancy is both patient and accommodating. Her basic price is $245 for black-and-white proofs or $295 for color proofs, with an additional charge for the prints selected. Prints cost $27.50 for black-and-white photos of any size, with duplicates $12 each. Color photos are $37.50 with duplicates $20 each (any size up to 11 x 14"). She will work in her studio or another location for an additional $150.

Devi Sanford*

802-8569

Devi will photograph your child in her studio, your home, or in an outdoor setting, such as Central Park. For a $200 sitting fee you get two rolls of black-and-white or color film (thirty-six exposures). Devi is a pleasure to work with; she trained with Annie Liebovitz.

A WORD ON PRESCHOOLS

As you begin to check out preschools—sometime between your child's first and second birthday—you will probably be subject to intermittent panic attacks. You'll hear rumors that this or that school is "hot" this year. You'll be baffled by the complexity of the admissions process. You'll feel as though you're trying to get an eighteen-year-old into Harvard, not a two-year-old into a sweet little place where she'll play and eat crackers and juice. Try to relax. Things will work out.

Here are some basic facts to keep in mind as you and your child march on toward preschool:

Many children begin preschool at age three or three and one-half years old; others begin as early as two years and four months old. Schools decide on cutoff ages for admission and often change these arbitrarily—a one-year-old born before March 15 can apply for admission for the following September; the next year, perhaps, a child born before March 31 can apply. Schools hold tight to their birth date policies, and there are few exceptions.

There are many excellent preschools in New York. Pick up a copy of the *Manhattan Directory of Private Nursery Schools* by Linda Faulhaber. This book describes all the private preschools in New York by neighborhood, with pertinent information from phone numbers to cutoff dates. Or look through the *New York*

Independent Schools Directory, published cooperatively by the Parents League and the Independent Schools Admission Association of Greater New York (available through the Parents League). But remember, there are excellent schools that are not members of the Parents League, and are therefore not listed in the League guidebook.

❋ As you begin your search, look for a school in your neighborhood. Try to keep your travel distance about ten blocks. Otherwise, you'll spend all your time getting there, when the school time itself is only two or three hours a day twice a week for children under three. Three-year-olds may go every day, and they'd rather spend their time at school than traveling to it.

❋ Talk to friends about their experiences with preschools. Make arrangements to visit the schools you're interested in; tours usually take place from October through January. You must call to make an appointment for a tour and/or request an application, the week of Labor Day. Some schools will not schedule a tour until they receive a completed applica-tion; others supply applications only after you have toured the school.

❋ Apply promptly. Schools have been known to stop sending applications by the last week of September, when they have already received enough applicants to fill their classes three times over. Apply to four or five schools. If you have a first choice, indicate it in a letter to the director of admissions of that particular school.

Your child will almost surely find a place in a preschool you like, and you will almost surely wonder a year from now what all the fuss was about.

Note: Each spring the 92nd Street Y offers a workshop called "Planning Your Child's Early School Years," conducted by Beth Teitelman and Barbara Katz who run the Parenting Center. The Parents League at 115 East 82nd Street (737-7385) runs one-on-one counseling sessions; they will give you the names and phone numbers of parents at various preschools who have agreed to talk to interested prospective parents.

PART TWO

shopping for a city baby:

everything you need to have

8 · maternity clothes

Whatever clothing your lifestyle demands, you can find it in New York's maternity stores. From Veronique Delachaux for unique and sophisticated clothes from France, to Mom's Night Out for the rental of a formal dress, to Mimi Maternity for a suit appropriate to the office, these stores offer all you need to stay comfortable and look great.

We shopped every maternity store in New York, and tried on dozens of items. We tested oversized and large-cut nonmaternity wear by well-known designers such as Joan Vass, Tapemeasure, Eileen Fisher, and Victoria's Secret. We discovered which designers make maternity lines, and which stores carry them.

If you're not much of a shopper, or if you're sticking to a budget, the Belly Basics Pregnancy Survival Kit can be a staple of your wardrobe from day one of your pregnancy. The kit includes leggings, a skirt, a long-sleeved tunic, and a baby doll dress, all of which are made of black cotton and lycra. You can mix and match the pieces or wear them with nonmaternity clothes. Kits are available at Bloomingdale's and Mimi Maternity for about $150; some pieces are sold separately. Pamela bought the leggings when she was pregnant with Benjamin and found them so comfortable she practically lived in them.

This chapter describes each New York maternity store—its focus, style, quality of merchandise, price range, and level of service. Most of these places hold their sales in January and July.

SHOPPING TIPS

Before you shop, here's some advice from two women who have learned by trial and error.

Hold off on buying maternity clothes for as long as you can. Remember, nine months is a long time, and you'll need new and different things as you grow bigger.

❋ In the first and second trimester, shop in regular clothing stores for larger sizes and items with elastic waists. The Gap, The Limited, and Victoria's Secret often offer inexpensive, machine-washable items with elastic waists. Buy large or extra large.

❋ Don't buy shoes in your first trimester; your feet will probably expand. Kelly had to buy two more pairs of shoes in her eighth month because she had only one pair that fit her.

❋ Buy fabrics you are used to and comfortable with. If you never wear polyester or rayon,

Top Eight Alternatives to Maternity Stores

1. Your husband's shirts and sweaters.
2. Borrow a friend's maternity clothes.
3. Eileen Fisher stores, where many styles are waistless, have elastic waist bands, and are cut full.
4. The jumpers and waistless dresses in Victoria's Secret catalogs are perfect, and affordable at $59 or less.
5. The Pregnancy Survival Kit.
6. Leggings and sweaters.
7. Rent it—check out Mom's Night Out.
8. Secondhand stores.

there's no need to start now. Stick to cotton or other natural fabrics that breathe, such as heavy-weight cotton blend suits you can wear when you go to a business meeting or out to dinner.

❋ Buy new bras, pantyhose, and maternity panties. You may go up as many as three cup sizes during your pregnancy, and bras with good support are essential. Maternity pantyhose by Hue and underwear by Japanese

Weekend are two of our favorites.

❋ For the last two months, invest in a maternity support belt, sold at every maternity store. The belt is a large, thick band of elastic that closes with Velcro under your belly to help hold it up. You will be able to walk more comfortably for longer periods of time.

❋ A pretty vest is an easy way to dress up an oxford shirt and a skirt or pair of leggings. Kelly loved to wear an oversized black turtleneck with black pants and a bright vest.

❋ Look in your husband's closet. A man's oxford shirt over a long elasticized skirt or leggings provides comfort and a clean, crisp look. Kelly bought some men's sweaters and shirts during her winter pregnancy—now her husband Carlo wears them.

THE STORES

A Pea in the Pod*

625 Madison Avenue at 59th Street

826-6468

Hours: Monday through Friday 10 A.M. to 7 P.M.; Saturday 10 A.M. to 6 P.M.; Sunday 12 P.M. to 6 P.M.

Return Policy: Store credit only.

This is a top-of-the line maternity store. It carries its own exclusive line and also commissions suits, dresses, and weekend wear by Carole Little, Joan Vass, David Dart, Shelli Segal, Lou Nardi, and Adrienne Vittadini. Amenities abound—big bathrooms, well-lit, extra-large dressing rooms with space to sit down, bottled water, toys for kids, and videos and magazines to occupy husbands and friends. The sales people are extremely helpful and are trained to fit you with the maternity and nursing bras you'll need. For working women, the store will set up after-hours appointments. Prices run in the $150 to $200 range for most designer pieces. Denim jeans are $58; leggings $29; and bras range from $18 to $50.

A Second Chance

1133 Lexington Avenue at 78th Street

744-6041

Hours: Monday through Friday 11 A.M. to 7 P.M.; Saturday 11 A.M. to 6 P.M.; Closed Sunday.

Return Policy: All sales are final.

A Second Chance offers used clothing for resale. Prices are about one quarter of the cost of a new item, and most of the pieces are in good shape. Although maternity wear is only a small segment of the inventory, the store stocks many basics you might be looking for. A Second Chance is hit or miss, so you'll probably have to go more than once.

Eileen Fisher

521 Madison Avenue at 53rd Street

759-9888

1039 Madison Avenue at 79th Street

879-7799

4341 Columbus Avenue at 76th Street

362-3000

103 Fifth Avenue at 17th Street

924-4777

Ninth Street at Second Avenue

(Outlet Store) 529-5715

Hours: Monday through Saturday 10 A.M. to 7 P.M.; Sunday 12 P.M. to 6 P.M.

Return Policy: Money is refunded within two weeks of purchase with a receipt; after two weeks a store credit is issued.

Eileen Fisher sells a range of wonderful full-cut separates, including elasticized pants with full legs, loose tunic-type sweaters, vests, and empire-waist dresses ($100 to $200). Most of it is machine washable. This is not a maternity store, but the clothing is perfect for your first or second trimester.

Madison Avenue Maternity and Baby

1043 Madison Avenue at 70th Street

988-8686

Hours: Monday through Friday 10 A.M. to 7 P.M.; Saturday 10 A.M. to 6 P.M.; Sunday 12 P.M. to 5 P.M.

Return Policy: Store credit only.

Madison Avenue Maternity imports most of its luxurious and stylish clothes—in beautiful cottons, wools, chenilles—from France and Italy. There are outfits for casual daytime wear ($100 and up), as well as dresses and suits appropriate for corporate life or a black-tie affair ($400 to $1,000). This store sells swimwear, underwear, and pantyhose, as well as lovely baby clothing.

Maternité by Mother's Work

1021 Third Avenue at 61st Street

832-2667

Hours: Monday through Friday 10 A.M. to 8 P.M.; Saturday and Sunday 11 A.M. to 6 P.M.

Return Policy: Store credit only.

Maternité by Mother's Work and Mimi Maternity are owned by the same company. You'll find more polyester and rayon at Mother's Work; more wool and silk at Mimi;

but prices run about the same in both stores (dresses average around $150). Mother's Work is a good bet for casual wear; leggings are reasonably priced, and sales provide substantial discounts.

Maternity Works Outlet

16-18 West 57th Street 399-9840

Hours: Monday through Wednesday 10 A.M. to 7 P.M.; Thursday 10 A.M. to 8 P.M.; Friday and Saturday 10 A.M. to 6 P.M.; Sunday 12 P.M. to 6 P.M.

Return Policy: Store credit only.

This second floor store is a clearinghouse for Mimi Maternity, Maternité by Mother's Work, and A Pea in the Pod. It features sale, off-season, and discontinued items all year round. If you don't mind sewing on a few buttons, there's also an "as is" and "sample" section with some real bargains—you just may find a $200 dress for $20. Check out Maternity Works Outlet if you're a midtown working-mom-to-be. You'll find everything from leggings and jeans to suits and coats.

Mimi Maternity*

1021 Third Avenue at 60th Street 755-2011

1125 Madison Avenue at 84th Street

737-3784

2005 Broadway at 69th Street 721-1999

2 World Financial Center 945-6424

Hours: Monday through Friday 10 A.M. to 7 P.M.; Saturday 12 P.M. to 6 P.M.; Sunday 10 A.M. to 6 P.M. Call the store nearest you to confirm hours.

Return Policy: Store credit only.

These stores carry a large and fashionable assortment of career suits, dresses (daytime and evening), and casual clothing by Mimi, Mother's Work, and Steena. Average prices: dresses, $150; a plain, elastic waist black skirt, $80; suits, $200. You'll also find an impressive selection of lingerie and sleepwear, including many top brand bras and panties (Olga, Japanese Weekend). A new addition to the store's private-label merchandise is the Mimi Bag ($148), which includes a black top, dress, skirt, and leggings, designed to be worn during and after pregnancy.

Mom's Night Out*

970 Lexington Avenue at 70th Street 744-6667

Hours: Monday through Friday 11 A.M. to 6 P.M.; Thursday until 8 P.M.; Saturday 11 A.M. to 5 P.M.;

Closed Sunday. Call for an appointment.
Return Policy: All the clothing is for rent and
must be returned. Some accessories may be
purchased.

Here's the place to rent formal evening
wear—short and long dresses, pant suits
and jackets—for one night or for a long weekend. Many of the dresses are designed by
owner Patricia Shiland, a former ready-to-
wear designer who adapts regular women's
formal styles to maternity wear. Prices range
from $65 to $145, and all the outfits are dry-
cleaned before rental. You can also find
accessories from a pearl choker to maternity
pantyhose. Friends of ours have used Mom's
Night Out with great success.

Motherhood Maternity
The Manhattan Mall
901 Avenue of the Americas
at 32nd Street 564-8170
1449 Third Avenue at 82nd Street
734-5984
444 Columbus Avenue at 82nd Street
799-0023
641 Avenue of the Americas
at 20th Street 741-3488
Hours: Monday through Saturday 10 A.M.
to 8 P.M.; Sunday 11 A.M. to 6 P.M.
Return Policy: Store credit only.

Motherhood Maternity carries a moderately priced line of maternity clothes many of
which are 100 percent rayon. The 32nd Street
store is small, but there are three large, well-lit
dressing rooms with good mirrors. The sales
staff tends to leave you on your own, which is
good if you're browsing. Prices are reasonable; most suits and dresses cost less than
$100. Jeans are $38; black leggings are $36;
and a stylish three-piece navy suit was $80
when we visited the store. Sweaters were
$49.99, marked down from $62.

Veronique Delachaux
1321 Madison Avenue at 93rd Street
831-7800
Hours: Monday through Saturday 10 P.M.
to 6 P.M.; Sunday 12 P.M. to 5 P.M.
Return Policy: Store credit only.

Veronique Delachaux carries its own chic
line of French-designed maternity wear. The
focus is on casual business attire: pants, blazers, and tops, with some special-occasion
items. The clothing is French–cut and may
not be suitable for women who wear large
sizes or who are very tall. The sales staff is

knowledgeable and helpful. Prices are steep; a suit usually costs more than $200 and a pair of jeans can be $80.

The Dan Howard Maternity Outlet
Route 4 West in Paramus, New Jersey, as well as other stores in Southern New Jersey and Long Island.
201-843-4980

Hours: Monday though Saturday 10 A.M. to 6 P.M.; Thursday 10 A.M. to 9 P.M.; closed Sunday.

This discount store carries clothes by Dan Howard. You'll find bargains here on sportswear such as leggings and T-shirts, as well as clothes for work. Not for the fashion-conscious working woman, but a good place for inexpensive wardrobe staples.

9 · baby furniture & accessories

Walk into a baby furniture store, and you face an unfamiliar sea of cribs, changing tables, and strollers. It's hard to imagine that a year from now you'll be an opinionated expert on all these items. We'll get you started with advice on what you need and why you need it, as well as the real facts about the distinctive merits of each product.

It's fun to plan for your baby's arrival, and we'll help you be smart about it. One of the most enjoyable parts is decorating your baby's room. While you're planning the decor, don't forget to make sure everything is baby-safe. Check here for tips and resources.

While cost and style will influence your choice of your baby's new stroller, crib, or changing table, New York mothers-to-be also have to consider space (as in, is your apartment a roomy two-bedroom plus dining room, or is it basically a large studio?) and portability (as in, do you have any idea how hard it is to maneuver a baby in a super-deluxe stroller in and out of a city bus or taxi?).

Don't run out and buy everything right away. You'll need the basics, such as a crib and stroller, but after that, wait until the baby is born. You may receive useful gifts. Also, try to borrow some things, such as bouncy seats and swings. When you are ready to shop, check out these listings—you're bound to find what you need. We list "baby super stores" which carry almost everything you need for a baby, from cribs to bibs to diapers to car seats. This information will give you an idea of what you want before you go shopping.

You might also wish to purchase the *Consumer Reports Guide to Baby Products*. This guide lists basic products by manufacturer and notes the pros and cons of each. While the information can sometimes seem outdated, you will be able to see pictures of some of the products you're interested in.

If you're of a mind (and pocketbook) to go all out and fix up a splendid room for your little one, New York has decorators and design consultants at your service. We interviewed a handful of interior designers who specialize in children's rooms. They can help with painting, wallpaper, and furniture decisions and they've also got great space-saving ideas for city apartments.

One bit of advice: Be sure to order your furniture at least twelve weeks before your due date. Kelly ordered her crib well in advance, and it still didn't arrive before Alexander did.

THE NECESSITIES
Bassinets

A bassinet is a lovely basket for a newborn to sleep in. It is usually used for about three months. It can be handy if you want your baby to sleep in your bedroom, or if a full-size crib seems too big for that tiny infant. These are the three most popular brands:

Badger. The Badger bassinet (and stand) retails from $50 to $130 and resembles a woven basket with a removable hood. There are a lot of styles—from bassinets with wheels, to those that rock, to those that lift off the stand. Badger is bigger than the Kids Line bassinet. You can use it longer before you switch to a crib, making it a good choice for a second baby who may be sleeping in your room for many months.

*Kids Line.** The Kids Line bassinet retails for $130 and features carry straps on the detachable basket for portability; a quilted liner; a coverlet; and a fitted sheet. The unit collapses for easy storage or travel and the bassinet linens (available in a variety of colors and patterns) are removable for washing.

Lee Hy. Lee Hy bassinets are plain and come in fewer styles than Kids Line, but they are also less expensive. Prices start at $50 and go up to about $100.

Century. The Bedside Bassinet has a basket under it. Prices range from $80 for basic white to $130 for one that includes linens.

Cribs

You have so many choices of styles, colors, and finishes, it's overwhelming. But there's no need to worry about safety. All cribs sold today are certified by the Juvenile Products Manufacturers Association (JPMA), which develops standards for many baby products, including strollers/carriages, highchairs, and playpens. JPMA safety specifications require that the space between crib bars is no more than two and three-eighths inches apart.

Here are the questions to ask when you shop for a crib:

Do both sides drop or only one?

✳ **Can you raise or lower the crib's sides with one hand while holding the baby, or do you need both hands? American–made cribs have metal kickstands under the side rails, making the sides easier to raise and lower. European cribs require two hands.**

✳ **How many mattress heights does the crib have? (Some cribs have only two levels—high for a newborn and low for a toddler—while other brands have a variety of heights).**

✳ **Is the crib stable when you shake it?**

The crib you bring home should have a mattress that fits snugly (a gap of no more than one and one-half inches between the mattress and the crib's sides and ends). Bumpers should be securely tied on with at least six ties or snaps. Keep the crib clear of any items—mobiles, clothing, toys—that have strings longer than seven inches. Don't set up the crib near any potential hazards in the room, such as a heater, window, or cords from blinds.

Below are the crib manufacturers whose products are widely available in the New York area. Shop around: prices range from $150 for a Bassett to more than $800 for a Bellini. Ask at each store whether they deliver and what they charge, and confirm they will assemble the crib in your home (they should).

Bassett. One of the best-looking affordable cribs on the market, Bassett is a good bet if you're on a tight budget or need a second crib at your in-law's house. Some are colorfully painted and others are made of

Nine Tips for a Baby's Room

1. Good overhead lighting is key for convenience and safety.
2. A humidifier can be important in overheated New York apartments.
3. Have as many dressers, drawers, or shelves as possible—you'll need them.
4. Design the closet in the baby's room to allow for more toy than clothing space; baby clothes are tiny.
5. Baby proof the room (see page 180).
6. Have some toys placed within your baby's reach.
7. A glider or rocker can save the day (or night).
8. Curtains or shades help baby sleep.
9. If possible, leave a play space in the middle of the room.

pretty wood. You'll find Bassett cribs at Toys "R" Us, Youngworld, and other Brooklyn stores. They are not widely available in Manhattan. The average price is $150.

Bellini. At $800 for some models, these handsome cribs in white-painted or natural wood are for splurge-minded parents only. They do have special features, such as a drawer underneath and multi-level mattress heights, and they can be converted into a toddler bed. Note: Raising or lowering a side requires two hands—not a plus. Cribs can be found only at Bellini stores.

Child Craft.* Made in the United States, these are among one of the most reasonably-priced ($200 to $400) cribs on the market. The cribs come in many styles, from contemporary to traditional, and are easy to use, with a side release mechanism you work with a kickstand.

Cosco. These cribs—found, like the Bassett, mostly in discount stores—are good looking, functional, and well-priced ($100 to $200). They are made of a lightweight metal, making them extremely portable, and some are available in bright colors.

Morigeau.* This Canadian crib is gaining popularity in New York. Morigeaus are stylish, and coordinating furniture is available in many different finishes. They feature an easy release mechanism; some cribs have single-sided drops. The price for a Morigeau ranges from $380 to $500.

Pali. These attractive Italian–made cribs retail for $400 to $500. They can be found at slightly discounted prices at the Baby and Toy Superstore in Stamford, Connecticut, and at Goldfinger's in Newark, New Jersey.

Ragazzi. These beautiful Canadian–made cribs ($350 to $500; crib and bed combination cost more) come in such unusual colors as forest green and burgundy as well as white and two-tone wood finishes. The brand is widely available in Manhattan and Brooklyn.

Simmons. * Simmons offers nearly thirty styles of cribs, priced from $200 to $400, with matching furniture. The cribs come in single-drop and double-drop styles, and the one-handed release mechanism is easy to use. Simmons is one of the few manufacturers to offer multiple mattress heights.

Changing Tables

Today's most popular changing tables are the flip-top dresser models. The top of the dresser becomes a changing area when you place the flip top, fitted with a pad, on top of the dresser. Remove the flip top once you're beyond the diaper stage, and you have a standard chest of drawers that's great for a toddler's room.

All the major baby furniture companies—Simmons, Child Craft, Morigeau, Bellini, and others—manufacture flip tops, which coordinate with the cribs they sell. Flip tops cost about $120 to $200.

Conventional changing tables have a little pad on top and shelves underneath for storing diapers and wipes. Popular brands include Gerry, Simmons, and Child Craft. Prices range from $99 to $200.

Gliders

A glider or rocking chair is optional, but if you have the space and the money, you'll love having one when you're feeding your baby or trying to get him to sleep. Family Home and Dutailier gliders retail for about $200 to $300 at baby super stores. They come in your choice of white or wood finishes, with different fabric patterns for the cushions. Dutailier offers options such as padded arms and decorator fabrics. Albee's, Bellini, and other super stores will custom-make a glider cover to match your decor.

Carriages/Strollers

Newborns and toddlers alike spend many hours in the stroller going to the park, the supermarket, or window-shopping along the avenues. New York is a walking town, and your stroller is the equivalent of a suburban minivan. Whether you choose a carriage (a bassinetlike construction on wheels) or a stroller (easily collapsible) depends on your personal needs. While suburban mothers and fathers may be content with an inexpensive umbrella stroller that spends most of its time in the trunk of a car, city parents know a sturdy carriage is a must-have for babies and toddlers, especially since we use it to carry the groceries home, too.

All strollers sold today are safe (the JPMA sees to that), but not every type may be right for you. Consider what time of year your baby is due before you purchase your carriage or stroller. For winter babies, a carriage with a boot (an enclosed end) might be the best bet to keep your infant warm. For summer babies, look for a carriage with good ventilation and a sunshade. Also consider where you live. If your building has a doorman, you can usually get some help carrying a heavier stroller up the stairs and inside. If you're in a walk-up or nondoorman building, look for one that's light and portable, and practice folding it to get it down to a quick routine;

you're going to be wrestling that stroller in and out of buses and cabs for a good couple of years.

Other desirable features include a stroller seat that reclines (a must for newborn to three-month-olds), plenty of storage space underneath, and brakes on all four wheels.

When preparing to buy, tell the store clerk how you plan to use the carriage, and ask for his recommendation. Take the carriage for a "test drive" in the store to see whether it feels comfortable for you and your husband; check the height of the handles or bar, and make sure neither of you has to hunch over to reach it comfortably.

Here are the carriages and strollers available in New York:

Aprica. These strollers are quite popular, especially the lightweight (seven and one-half pounds) Flash stroller that folds with one hand (retails for around $189 at the superstores). Other models are the Super Zap and the Windsor. Pam used a Flash (formerly the City Mini) and loved it for its size and ease of use.

Century. Century makes a number of different strollers, with prices ranging from $20 to $150. Their most exciting product is the 4-

in-1 Car Seat stroller ($150), which combines the Century infant car seat with a lightweight metal base and serves as a carriage/stroller and car seat. We wouldn't recommend the 4-in-1 as your only stroller, but you'll find it has its uses. Kelly bought the base only (sold in The Right Start catalog) to use with her Century infant car seat when she went traveling with Alexander. She found it easy to wheel him around the airport instead of carrying him in the heavy car seat.

Chicco. These Italian-made strollers look similar to the Combi Savvy, a lightweight umbrella stroller, but are less expensive ($120 to $150). They weigh ten pounds, and have three positions (so that baby can nap more comfortably).

Combi.* The Combi Savvy is another popular umbrella/lightweight stroller. The Savvy weighs less than eight pounds and is fairly easy to fold (not as easy as the Aprica Flash, but easier than most). This stroller comes with a full canopy and a storage basket and reclines for napping. It is available in a number of attractive patterns (approximately $189).

Emmaljunga. These beautiful, English-style prams (made in Sweden), have old-fashioned contouring and are sturdy, heavy, and built to last. The Emmaljunga features oversized wheels, a shock absorber system, a five-point harness, and a chrome chassis. Make sure you have room in your apartment, as these strollers do not fold up easily for storage. They retail for $250 to $450.

Gerry. Gerry is best known for its Roller Baby jogging stroller, very popular with parents who exercise with their babies. The Roller Baby is well constructed and folds up to fit in your closet or car trunk. It retails for $200. A marathon runner we know has used this stroller to run with his daughter for three years, ever since she was three months old.

Graco. Graco makes a reasonably priced stroller/carriage sold at some of the super stores and at mass-market retailers like Toys "R" Us. A complete carriage for a newborn—with a storage basket, a boot, and a three-position reclining seat—can be found for $100.

Inglesina. Inglesina is known for its double (and triple) stroller, so if twins are in your future, or you're going to have a baby *and* a toddler in tow, check it out. These Italian-made strollers are attractive, large, built to last, and have excellent under-carriage storage space. They retail from $200 to $300.

Maclaren. Most retailers agree that the Maclaren is the most durable lightweight umbrella stroller available today. Maclarens, made in England, consistently have the lowest rate of returns or repairs and have withstood the test of time for parents who re-use them with their second child. They come in a variety of weights (eight, ten, and twelve pounds), and some models have sun canopies and reclining seats. Although not quite as easy to fold as the Aprica Flash, their folding mechanism is simple. They retail for $170. The Maclaren double stroller is popular for twins and for an older toddler and a baby. Our friends with two children prefer the Maclaren.

Peg Perego. It is generally agreed that the Peg Perego strollers are the best of the lot for a full carriage/stroller. We both have the Milano ($320) and love it. These Italian-made strollers are so popular in New York, the playgrounds look like Peg Perego parking lots! They are sturdy, attractive, stand folded upright for storage, and have a multitude of features that make life easy for mom and baby (reversible handle, large removable storage basket, full boot, and large canopy). The most popular styles are the Milano, the Roma, and the Pliko, a lighter weight stroller.

Car Seats

Even if you don't have a car, you should have a car seat. To start with, state law dictates that your newborn must leave the hospital in one. And while you can borrow a seat from a friend, purchasing your own will be a practical investment.

By law, in any automobile, babies must always ride in a car seat. City taxis must come equipped with rear seat belts to attach over the baby seat, so double check before you get into a cab. If you have any questions, call the New York Coalition for Transportation Safety at 516-829-0099. That said, it's very difficult to carry both a car seat and a stroller around with you. Instead, most New York parents use a baby carrier for infants, and hold toddlers on their laps.

There are two ways to go with car seats, but experts advise you to buy an infant car seat (good for babies up to twenty pounds) and later a full-sized toddler seat. The alternative is a convertible car seat that can be used from birth through the toddler years. Infant car seats, however, are smaller, recline better, often come with a sunshade, and are more heavily padded than the convertible. They're portable and can easily be carried in and out of the car without disturbing a sleeping baby. Remember that these seats must be rear-facing in your vehicle; toddler seats forward-facing.

Three designs of restraining straps or harnesses are available in car seats: the five-point harness, the T-shield, and the bar shield. Most experts agree that the five-point harness is the safest, but all three are considered to be safe. The five-point harness is also the most time-consuming to put on and off, which can be annoying to impatient toddlers. All of this will make sense once you see them in the stores. The best-sellers in Manhattan and Brooklyn are Century and Evenflo car seats.

Century. * The Century Smart Fit (which replaced the 590) is the newest and most popular Century car seat. The seat comes with a base that can be strapped into your car and left there. The seat can also be used without the base. These seats are easy to work and can't be beat for portability. They retail at $80 but can be found for less at Toys "R" Us and Yeedl's in Brooklyn.

Century also makes some models that convert to toddler seats. Some are available with a five-point harness, others with a bar shield. The Century Smart Move is the newest convertible car seat and is for infants up to forty-pound children.

Evenflo. Evenflo car seats are very popular, especially the deluxe Medallion and the Ultara ($110), which is the most widely available convertible seat and comes with a five-point harness, pillow and cushions, and a three-position reclining mode. Albee's highly recommends the Medallion for babies over twenty pounds. Retailers also endorse the On My Way infant car seat which is used only with its base.

Baby Swings

A baby swing might be your lifesaver during your baby's first few months. Or not. This is something your child either loves or hates. (Rebecca hated it, so the swing sat idle in the middle of Pamela's living room for five months. Alexander loved it and never cried when he was in it.) We recommend you borrow one from a friend or relative before making the investment.

Graco. The Graco Swyngomatic is the only widely available swing. It's great. There are two models on the market—with and without the overhead bar. The benefit of the Graco Advantage is that it has no bar on which you might accidentally hit your baby's head. Graco Advantage retails for $100; the original Graco can be found for $40 to $80.

Bouncy Seats

The bouncy seat is another lifesaver; in fact, we know many women who would not have been able to shower for six months if they had not been able to put the baby in this safe spot. It's portable; you can move it from the living room to the kitchen to the bathroom so that you can always see your baby and he can always see you. The bouncy seat is also great for feeding your baby when he's starting to eat solid food but is still too small for a highchair. Here's a list of the bouncy seats available in New York:

Baby Bjorn. The Baby Bjorn bouncy seat has four reclining positions and can be used for children up to age two. But at $99, it's a bit expensive for something that's always spit up on. (And no matter how comfortable it is, we can't imagine any two-year-old staying happily strapped into any seat.)

Summer.* Summer is to bouncy seats what Band-Aids are to adhesive strips. These attractive seats are reasonably priced (from $29 for a plain one to $48 for a seat with a head rest and removable toy), lightweight, portable, and machine washable.

Hoohobbers.* Hoohobbers is the trendsetter of bouncy seats. It looks similar to the Summer seat but is more like a mini rocking chair—the base is curved, making it easy for a child to rock himself. It comes with a sun shield, and the top-of-the-line model has a play bar that can be attached. Hoohobbers are available in a variety of beautiful patterns and prints; they cost between $65 and $75.

Highchairs

When you are buying a highchair, it is advisable to:

1. **Buy a chair with a wide base to limit the chances of the chair tipping over.**
2. **Find a chair with an easy, one-hand tray release mechanism, which makes it easier to take your baby in and out.**

Most highchair accidents occur (usually with children under one year) when a child has not been strapped in properly and then tumbles out. Don't rely on the chair's tray to keep your baby enclosed; use the safety belt.

Despite all the sleek, modern-looking,

multi-feature highchairs on the market (in metal and vinyl), what's hot now are unencumbered wood highchairs. These attractive chairs, made by Rochelle and Union City (found at Ben's), appeal to parents who want a look that fits their decor and who aren't as concerned with ease in handling and cleaning.

Whatever you're looking for, you'll find it. Here are some of the most popular brands:

Baby Trend.* The Baby Trend Home and Roam highchair is available at Albee's and through The Right Start catalog. It is an excellent choice for many reasons, including its thickly padded seat that can adjust to six different heights, and its wraparound tray (not found on many other highchairs and a great feature for messy eaters). In addition, the seat can be taken off to become a portable hook-on chair for taking to restaurants or attaching to your own table. It costs about $100.

Gerry. The Gerry Adjust-A-Height model (adjusts to five height levels) is one of the country's best-sellers, but it's not very popular in New York, perhaps because of its less-than-stylish patterns. These chairs are reasonably priced; $65 at Toys "R" Us.

Peg Perego.* The Peg Perego highchair is similar to the Baby Trend Home and Roam with six height adjustments, a thickly padded seat, and a wide base. The tray has a one-handed release but does not wrap around the chair. It's also more expensive ($119 at Toys "R" Us; $139 at Ben's for Kids). The newest, most deluxe model, Prima Pappa, features a reclining seat ($175). The Peg Perego comes in a variety of pretty patterns and is hands-down the best-seller in many stores.

Rochelle. Rochelle wood highchairs are traditional looking, stylish, and can fit easily into any decor. These chairs do not have many of the features of the Peg Perego or Baby Trend—the height cannot be adjusted, the tray is smaller, and the chair is more difficult to clean—but if aesthetics are important and space is an issue, the Rochelle highchair may be just the one for you. It retails for approximately $139.

Another model available at Ben's For Kids and Baby Palace is the Chicco highchair, which looks similar to the Peg Perego. The Chicco is attractive and functional but hasn't been available long enough to have a real track record.

Booster Seats/Hook-On Seats

You may want to buy a portable chair to use when you take your baby or toddler to a restaurant or other place where no highchair is available.

Hook-on seats have a short life (Rebecca couldn't sit comfortably in one after she was nine months old). These seats have also caused many accidents with children under the age of one, occurring when the seat was incorrectly hooked to the table or when the child detached the seat from under the table with his foot. If you do use a hook-on seat, always place a chair under it. Sassy is the most popular brand sold and has the best rating from Consumer Reports.

We have found booster seats to be safer and more practical than hook-ons. They can be used for children up to preschool age, and our favorite, the Safety 1st, can be easily folded.

Dolly Go 'n' Grow. This seat was rated the safest in Consumer Reports but we could only find it at Albee's. It has two types of restraints and an adjustable backrest and seat.

Safety 1st.* This brightly-colored seat is becoming very popular. It has two restraining straps, one that attaches the seat to the chair, and one to strap your child in. The chair is sturdy, easy to clean, and best of all, it folds easily for transport. It retails for $30.

Playpens/Portable Cribs

Playpens are a great place to park your baby when you need five minutes to yourself to shower, answer the door, talk on the phone, or make dinner. Some babies might amuse themselves in the playpen for up to thirty minutes at a time. But playpens are big and difficult to store and transport, so you might want to go for the portable crib instead. It can function as a playpen, but it's smaller and can easily be put away. Portable cribs have a thin mattress and sheets, so they can be used as a crib when you're traveling.

Brevi.* Brevi is the most popular (and often only) brand of traditional playpen sold in New York. These pens are attractive, fold easily, and are spacious enough for baby but small enough not to take over your entire apartment. Kelly used a Brevi for about fifteen months. Alexander used to sit in it and play for just about the time it took his mom to shower, dress, and make the bed. They are priced at about $130.

Evenflo Happy Camper. This mesh portable crib/playpen looks identical to the Graco Pack 'N Play but is not as easy to fold, and the patterns are louder. At $100, it's less expensive than the Pack 'N Play. Evenflo also makes the Cabana, which is designed especially for outdoor use and has a removable roof.

Graco Pack 'N Play.* Graco introduced the soft, mesh, portable crib, which is the easiest to use. It comes in a variety of styles: a standard playpen (retailing for $120); one with a bassinet insert; and one with shades to block out the light falling on a sleeping baby. Graco gets high marks from *Consumer Reports* as well as mothers.

Century and Fisher-Price also make portable cribs, but neither brand is widely available in New York.

Bathtubs/Bath Seats

At first, bathe your tiny baby in the kitchen or bathroom sink. When he's a little bigger and you'd prefer to use the bathtub, you may want to buy a special baby tub that fits into the big tub. Most baby tubs are similar; they come either with or without a sponge insert. We opt for without, because the sponge tends to get that awful mildew odor, is hard to wring out, and takes days to dry.

When your baby is old enough to sit up on his own, he's ready for a bath seat.

Fisher-Price. The Fisher-Price bathtub ($19) is great for either a large single or double sink, or a bathtub. It has an attached drain plug, and the angled side of the seat has a cushioned, mildew-resistant pad.

Gerry.* The bestselling Gerry Two-Year tub is the sturdiest of tubs and can be used for a child up to two years old. It has an insert for infants up to three months old, which can easily be removed as the child grows. It retails for $20. The Gerry bath seat or ring fits into your tub and has suction cups on the bottom. The front part folds down for ease in getting your baby in and out.

Safety 1st.* The Safety 1st bath seat ($15) is a ring, like the Gerry seat, that attaches to your bathtub with suction cups. It is roomy enough to hold a two-year-old. We have both been happy with the Safety 1st.

Sassy. This inflatable tub is relatively inexpensive ($9). Deflate it after each use, and you don't have to have a tub lying around the bathroom or kitchen.

Baby Carriers

You see these pouchlike, soft cloth carriers strapped onto the fronts of mothers and fathers everywhere. They're often called "snuglis" for the company that invented them. While the actual Snuglis are attractive and functional, they have been surpassed in quality and price by Baby Bjorn. Pamela's Snugli went virtually unused for Rebecca, but a friend gave her a Baby Bjorn when Benjamin was born, and she uses it every day.

This is another item that you'll use for only a short time. Kelly purchased one and then had a nine and one-half pound baby, who quickly became too heavy to carry strapped onto her shoulders. Try to borrow one from a friend and test it with your baby before purchasing to see if you're comfortable with it.

Baby Bjorn.* The Baby Bjorn, the best-selling carrier in New York, comes in attractive colors like navy blue, forest green, and black. It straps on and off easily. At $69, it is more expensive than the Snugli, but we (and other moms we know) agree that it's worth the price if you plan to use a baby carrier often.

Nojo. Nojo, another popular brand, is widely available at the super stores. The most well-known model is the Baby Sling, which retails for about $40. With the Baby Sling, you can hold your baby either in the usual vertical position or horizontally, which may allow your child to sleep more comfortably and makes nursing easier.

Sara's Ride.* The Sara's Ride is a carrier for babies who are at least four months old and able to hold their heads upright. Its patented waist belt helps distribute the weight of the baby to your hips rather than on your shoulders and back. Mothers who use the Sara's Ride love it and say it's great for taking your baby shopping or on the subway or bus without a stroller. It retails for about $30.

Snugli. The Snugli is the grandmother of the category, but we find it somewhat less durable and more difficult to use than the Baby Bjorn. Snuglis come in various styles; the Legacy converts from an upright carrier to a cradle style. It sells for about $50.

Backpacks

Women who use backpacks swear by them for comfort and convenience. Your baby is ready for a backpack once she can sit up on her own. Borrow one from a friend, and try it out with your baby on board before you decide to purchase your own.

The two most popular brands are Gerry and Tough Travelers. The Gerry backpack is lightweight and retails for $65 to $130, depending on the model. Tough Travelers is a heavy-duty backpack that can be used for hiking with baby in tow. It retails for $80 to $130.

Baby Monitors

Here's how to be in one room and hear your baby crying in another. These gadgets give you lots of options. Some monitors are battery-operated and can be carried throughout the apartment. The newest model on the market is BabyCam, which features a wireless camera and TV screen monitor system to let you see and hear your baby from up to one hundred feet away. It retails for $325. The best and most widely available are:

Fisher-Price. * The Fisher-Price Sound and Lights Monitor is recommended at most super stores; in fact, it is the only brand sold at Ben's for Kids and at Baby Palace. The monitor has two channels so that if one is picking up static, you can easily switch to the other. Lights on the receiver signal in the dark that your baby is crying. It sells for $70. Pamela

has used this monitor for over three years without a problem.

The Sony Baby Call is also a popular model; it retails for $75.

Diaper Bags

Diaper bags come in two basic styles: over-the-shoulder, which zips or snaps closed, and a knapsack with a drawstring opening.

You won't believe how much stuff you have to carry for your baby. Find a roomy bag with lot of pockets (for bottles, wipes and the like) and a plastic lining. A changing pad is another great feature. The super stores have terrific selections. Babies Alley makes a popular Chanel look-alike, in quilted black with gold chain straps. Peg Perego has patterns that match their carriages. Pierre Deux's pretty (and functional) bag comes in a variety of colors. Chic handbag designer Kate Spade has gotten into the act and has designed two styles—in basic black, of course! Other newcomers to the diaper bag market include Molehill and Baby Mania; the models are quite stylish and don't even look like diaper bags. They're at Baby Palace. Prices range from $20 for a Babies Alley diaper bag to $200 for a Pierre Deux. You decide.

THE STORES

Our baby super stores are not necessarily large in size, but we consider them super because they provide one-stop shopping. Here you can buy all the furniture you need (crib, changing table, dresser), as well as sheets, towels, diapers, nipples, bottles, layettes or clothing for newborns, strollers/ carriages, highchairs, playpens, baby carriers/ knapsacks, and much, much more. You get the idea. We like them because they make your life easy. Most sell toys, too, but be aware that the selection is limited and the prices are often higher than at Toys "R" Us or other toy stores.

Some stores are ritzier than others, some more value oriented. The proximity of the store to your home should help you decide where to shop. Many expectant moms in New York visit too many stores in their quest for the perfect crib, sheets, and towels. You don't have to! Find a place that's convenient, and use it for all your needs. We've found that when you patronize one store consistently, the staff gets to know you and will go the extra mile when necessary. We have also discovered it is wise to buy in bulk. Many stores never officially discount but may still give you a better price if you are placing a large order. Don't be afraid to ask. And there's no harm in asking if they'll match the better price you've seen somewhere else.

Also check out the store's delivery policy. Policies vary widely.

Super Stores

Albee's*

715 Amsterdam Avenue at 95th Street
662-8902
Hours: Monday, Tuesday, Wednesday, Friday, and Saturday 9 A.M. to 5.30 P.M.; Thursday 9 A.M. to 7:30 P.M.; Closed Sunday.
Return Policy: Refunds with receipt.

Albee's is not glamorous—fluorescent lighting, no carpeting, and lots of chaos give you an idea of the atmosphere—but we love it. Carla, Ari, and Michael, the owners, are friendly, knowledgeable, and down-to-earth. We also appreciate their honesty. Pamela was talked out of purchasing a slew of newborn sleepers that Carla said the baby would outgrow in a month. (She was right!) Prices here are the best in the city on many items including highchairs, playpens, and strollers. Yet it's not for the faint of heart. Albee's is always busy and so fully stocked that you have to navigate carefully. They carry Simmons, Child Craft, and Morigeau cribs, as well as some Ragazzi and Lexington brands and all the carriage/stroller brands. What they don't have in stock, they can order for you. Albee's also sells clothing, bedding, nipples, bottles, bottle racks, carriage accessories, tapes, videos, books, bibs, and diaper bags, but not diapers or formula.

Baby Depot

116 West 23rd Street 229-1300
Hours: Monday through Saturday:
9 A.M. to 9 P.M.; Sunday 10 A.M. to 6 P.M.
Return Policy: Store credit only.

Baby Depot is part of Burlington Coat Factory, a huge store at 23rd Street and Sixth Avenue. It carries everything you'll want, including cribs, highchairs, strollers, clothes, and more. All the prices are good. Baby Depot carries a large selection of Simmons and Child Craft cribs. Their stroller selection includes Peg Perego, Aprica, Graco, Combi, and Kolcraft. Baby Depot offers a nice selection of books and videos for babies and toddlers as well as all the accessories such as nipples and bottles, bibs, cups, and spoons. Their clothing selection is decent, and they have good prices on Carter's.

The Baby Palace*

1410 Lexington Avenue at 92nd Street
426-4544
Hours: Monday through Thursday 10:30 A.M. to 7 P.M.; Friday 10:30 A.M. to before sundown between 2:30 P.M. and 5 P.M.; Closed Saturday; Sunday 11 A.M. to 5 P.M.
Return Policy: Furniture, special orders, and sale items are final sale. Gifts and other items in perfect condition may be exchanged and in some cases a refund may be issued.

A fixture in Chelsea for seven years, this clean, bright store, owned by the helpful Herman Cziment, recently moved to the Upper East Side. Baby Palace carries many of the better brands. Crib choices include Simmons, Child Craft, Morigeau, and C&T, and range from $200 to $500. In strollers/carriages, they carry Peg Perego, Maclaren, Combi, and Emmaljunga. You'll also find bumper sets, books, videos, stuffed animals, layette clothing, and bottles. There is a nice selection of toys for infants and smaller babies, including Ambi, Battat, Early Start, and Safety 1st. A baby registry is available. Prices are excellent. Weekday delivery is free of charge for Manhattan; $15 for Brooklyn and Queens.

Bellini

1305 Second Avenue at 68th Street
517-9233
110 West 86th Street 580-3801
*Hours: Monday through Friday 10 A.M.
to 6 P.M.; Thursday 10 A.M. to 8 P.M.; Saturday
10 A.M. to 5:30 P.M.; Sunday 12 P.M. to 5 P.M.*
Return Policy: Store credit.

Customers who shop here rave about the top of the line furniture and service at this Tiffany's of baby stores. Bellini provides parents-to-be with the longest list of baby necessities we've ever seen! The staff will spend hours helping you select the perfect crib (this is the only place in town to find a Bellini crib) and coordinating furniture and bedding. They custom-make bedding sets and have a library of fabrics you can choose from. You'll find a good selection of strollers/carriages, including Peg Perego, Combi, and Maclaren. Special knit items like sweaters and christening outfits are exquisite. Kelly got a wonderfully trimmed receiving blanket from Bellini with a matching diaper and bib. Delivery is $50 for a crib, $10 to $15 for smaller items (delivered by messenger). They say they will match prices if they can verify what another store charges.

Ben's for Kids*

1380 Third Avenue at 78th Street 794-2330
*Hours: Monday through Friday 10 A.M.
to 5 P.M.; Thursday 10 A.M. to 8 P.M.; Saturday
11 A.M. to 5 P.M.; Closed Sunday.*
Return Policy: Refund with receipt, otherwise store credit. Merchandise must be in salable condition and in the original boxes.

Ben's for Kids, a pretty and comforting store with a very helpful staff, was recently named one of the top twenty specialty stores in the United States by *Small World* magazine. Don and Madeline Wein work hard to keep it top-notch. Ben's for Kids has a modest selection of cribs, a larger selection of strollers and highchairs, and all the accessories and paraphernalia you could ever want. When Kelly went in looking for a bottle sterilizer after Alexander was born, Don convinced her she didn't really need one. He was right. Ben's sells cribs by Simmons, Child Craft, C & T International, and Ragazzi. The strollers/carriages include Peg Perego, Emmaljunga, Aprica, Graco, Combi, Inglesina, Maclaren, and Chicco. Shop here for kiddy clothing too, up to size 4T. Ben's for Kids delivers five days a week and usually guarantees next day delivery if the item is in stock.

Delivery is free in New York; they ship UPS outside the city. Upper East Siders love Ben's for its quality, service, and selection.

Schneider's

20 Avenue A at Houston Street 228-3540
Hours: Monday through Saturday 10 A.M. to 6 P.M.; Sunday 11 A.M. to 5 P.M.
Return Policy: Refund with receipt, otherwise store credit only.

Schneider's is a true neighborhood store, and downtown parents couldn't survive without it. A tradition on the Lower East Side for years, this is the only baby super store in the East or West Village. The staff is helpful, and the store sells cribs such as Simmons and Child Craft, and carriages/strollers made by Maclaren, Peg Perego, and Graco. Schneider's will also repair strollers of most makes and models. It carries a full line of accessories, such as pacifiers, safety items, and bottles, but no clothing.

Toys "R" Us

Broadway at 34th Street 594-8697
Hours: Monday through Saturday 9 A.M. to 8 P.M.; Sunday 11 A.M. to 7 P.M.
24-30 Union Square East 674-8697

Hours: Monday through Saturday 9 A.M. to 9 P.M.; Sunday 10 A.M. to 7 P.M.
Return Policy: Refund with receipt, otherwise store credit only.

We love Toys "R" Us. They sell furniture and accessories at the best prices in town. You'll find cribs for under $200, strollers, highchairs, playpens, bottles, bibs, waterproof bed pads, as well as diapers and formula (available by the case). While Toys "R" Us favors the mass-market labels, you can find some of the better brands such as Peg Perego and Graco, plus Cosco, Kolcraft, Gerry, Aprica, and Fisher-Price. Everything is self-serve, and there's no delivery, so you'll have to wrestle the large ticket items out of the store on your own. Weekdays and evenings are your best bet for shopping; these stores are mobbed on the weekends.

Specialty Stores

ABC Carpet & Home

888 Broadway at 19th Street 473-3000
Hours: Monday through Friday 10 A.M. to 8 P.M.; Saturday 10 A.M. to 7 P.M.; Sunday 11 A.M. to 6:30 P.M.
Return Policy: Refund with receipt, otherwise store credit only.

Style-conscious parents need not worry about outfitting their little one's room. ABC Carpet and Home stocks a small but carefully chosen selection of nursery furnishings in keeping with its antique and country chic theme. The look here is handmade, sophisticated rustic, evoking the nineteenth century. You'll find everything from Victorian-inspired cast iron cribs and cradles to fashionably distressed decorative accessories. In addition to home furnishings, there is an impressive selection of high quality baby and toddler clothing, a huge range of plush and classic toys, and children's books and stationery. This is an excellent spot to pick up gifts.

Pamela Scurry's Wicker Garden

1327 Madison Avenue at 92nd Street
410-7001
Hours: Monday through Saturday 10 A.M.
to 6 P.M.; Closed Sunday.
Return Policy: Store credit only.

This top-of-the-line boutique is exquisite, and the baby furniture, much of which is hand-painted, is some of the loveliest in town. You'll find finishing touches, such as coordinating wastepaper baskets, diaper pails, chests, and changing tables to match a crib. They have books of linens to choose from, will custom-make anything, and also carry top brands such as Blauen. The main floor has a full layette selection; most of the clothing is imported from France and Italy, all with the Wicker Garden label. This is the place for beautiful children's clothes when you choose to go first class.

Portico Kids

1167 Madison Avenue at 86th Street
717-1963
Hours: Monday through Saturday 10 A.M.
to 6 P.M.; Sunday 12 P.M. to 5 P.M.
Return Policy: Store credit only.

This exclusive furniture store sells beautiful things—much of it custom made and hand painted. We hear that many celebrities have outfitted their children's rooms from Portico Kids. There's a strong selection of twin beds for toddlers, and you'll find a selection of ready-made crib and linen sets. You can custom order anything you want. Special orders take at least ten to twelve weeks, so order early.

Super Stores Outside of New York

The Baby and Toy Superstore*

11 Forest Street, Stamford, CT 06901
203-327-1333

Hours: Monday, Tuesday, Wednesday, Friday, and Saturday 9:30 A.M. to 5:30 P.M.; Thursday 9:30 A.M. to 8 P.M.; Sunday 12 P.M. to 5 P.M.
Return Policy: Refund within fifteen days with a receipt, otherwise store credit only.

The store is clean, bright, and big, and offers all the best brands at possibly the best prices around. Roz, Neil, and Seth Berger, the owners, work closely with customers. Cribs include Morigeau, Simmons, Child Craft, Pali, and Ragazzi. Strollers include Peg Perego, Combi, Maclaren, Aprica, Emmaljunga, and Inglesina. They sell ready-made linens, but will custom-make beautiful crib sets as well. New York residents pay no tax, but there is an $80 delivery charge, which you may be able to negotiate. You may realize significant savings if you buy all your baby furniture here. Kelly loves Baby and Toy Superstore.

Darling's

137 E. Post Rd, White Plains, NY 10601
914-949-6777
169 South Central Avenue
Hartsdale, NY 10530 914-993-0800
Hours: Monday through Saturday 10 A.M. to 5 P.M.; Closed Sunday.
Return Policy: Refund with receipt within seven days, otherwise store credit only.

Our friends in Westchester recommend this store, which has infant and baby clothing, furniture, toys, strollers, car seats, playpens, and more. Prices are good, and the staff is friendly and helpful. Darling's carries cribs by Simmons, Child Craft, Morigeau, Bassett, and many of the Italian imports, including Pali and Tracer. They also have a large stroller selection, including Peg Perego, Maclaren, Graco, Aprica, and Gerry. The White Plains store is bigger than the Hartsdale location, but both carry much of the same merchandise. Darling's has a full layette department, clothing for children up to two years old, and a baby registry. They will special order furniture and accessories they don't stock. Delivery to New York is $25.

Goldfinger's

174 Ferry Street, Newark, NJ 07105
201-344-6900
Hours: Monday, Wednesday, and Friday 9:30 A.M. to 9 P.M.; Tuesday, Thursday, and Saturday 9:30 A.M. to 6 P.M.; Closed Sunday.
Return Policy: Refund within thirty days with a receipt; otherwise store credit only.

Goldfinger's just might be the largest

baby store in the tri-state area. In each product category, a majority of big manufacturers are represented, and Goldfinger's has the most extensive selection of cribs and matching furniture we have seen. Cribs are made by Simmons, Morigeau, Childcraft, Polly, C & T, Tracer, Bassett and Kolcraft. Goldfinger's makes custom bedding sets, which cost between $300 and $600. They carry the "crib in a bag" (which includes bumpers, a comforter, a sheet, and a dust ruffle). Layette brands include Absorba, Baby Dior, Mini Clasix, Gerber, Carter's, Petit Bateau, Little Me, and Guess. They carry christening and bris outfits as well. New York residents must pay a three percent sales tax. Delivery every day but Sunday.

INTERIOR DESIGN AND DECORATION

Ready to get creative? The following New York stores sell children's wallpapers, borders, and accessories to help you pull together your baby's room. Many have in-store consultants with experience or degrees in interior design. We have also listed a few interior designers who specialize in children's rooms. We have seen their work, and it is truly special.

Gracious Home
1220 Third Avenue at 70th Street
517-6300

Gracious Home sells beautiful coordinated borders, wallpaper, and paint. They also have area rugs, wastepaper baskets, lamps, bathroom accessories, and more. They will make up any window treatment you desire, or coordinate an entire room. The entire selection is quite beautiful.

Janovic Plaza*
1150 Third Avenue at 67th Street 772-1400
159 West 72nd Street 595-2500
771 Ninth Avenue at 52nd Street 245-3241
215 Seventh Avenue at 22nd Street 645-5454

Janovic Plaza offers wallpaper, borders, paints, and window treatments, and designers there will help plan your room and coordinate everything. There's a nice selection of reasonably priced fabrics suitable for a child's room. Ask about Janovic's classes on painting and wallpapering. Pamela has used the Janovic Plaza store on West 72nd Street for borders and window treatments, with happy results.

Laura Ashley Home

398 Columbus Avenue at 79th Street

496-5110

In their Mother and Child collection, Laura Ashley offers complete bedding ensembles to match window treatments, lamp shades, wastepaper baskets, diaper stackers, and more. Check out their Humpty Dumpty and Hey Diddle Diddle rooms. Laura Ashley has one of the best border selections around; everything is premade and ready to go. Several times a year, custom-made bedding and window treatments are available at reduced prices when you purchase a full-priced fabric.

Plain Jane

525 Amsterdam Avenue at 85th Street

595-6916

Hours: Monday through Saturday 11:00 A.M. to 6 P.M.; Closed Sunday.

Return Policy: Store credit only.

If you want to put together a 40s/50s retro look, this eclectic store sells decorative accessories and bedding for the home, especially for a baby's room (which, of course, is exactly what you're looking for). They do a wonderful job with custom bedding, and have a knack for arranging items in displays that will give you lots of ideas.

Kids Digs

Carol Maryan

215 West 79th Street, #1A 787-7800

Owner Carol Maryan is an architect and designer who specializes in child-oriented spaces. Her room designs can be adapted to your child's needs as the years go by. A consultation, which is a problem-solving session and includes a sketch of the proposed room, is $350. Carol will complete a design project at an hourly rate of $90.

Smart Start

Susan Weinberg

334 West 86th Street, Suite 6C 580-4924

Susan, a designer/architect, starts with a list of your basic needs, then helps you select furniture. She will even shop for you. A consultation is $100 in the city; $150 outside the city. Her hourly rate is $100; for large projects, her fee is twenty percent of the cost. She can also help with bris or christening celebrations and will order birth announcements.

Charm and Whimsy*

Esther Sadowky

114 East 23rd Street 683-7609

Esther is an interior designer with a talent for turning small spaces into something special. She has created, for example, a covered wagon bed for a Western-themed boy's room and a custom dollhouse for a little girl's room. She can design furniture, select fabrics and carpeting, and hand-paint your chairs and benches. She can even paint a mural on your child's ceiling; the cost is $500 for a mural with a simple image.

Funtastic Interiors, Inc.

Kimberly Fiterman, A.S.I.D.

60 West 12th Street 633-0660

Kimberly has a library of resources and has designed nurseries, bedrooms, and playrooms for children of all ages. Her rate is $100 an hour or thirty percent of an established budget.

BABY PROOFING

Little did you know your apartment is a danger zone. But beware if you have—as do most of us—a glass or sharp-edged coffee table, electrical outlets, lamps, lamp cords, drawers, cleaning solutions under sinks/vanities, or anything sitting on a table. Baby proofing your home is one of the most important tasks you'll undertake. By the time your child begins to creep and crawl, all potentially dangerous objects must be covered, secured, removed, or replaced.

Here are three ways to get baby proofing help:

Buy a book or video such as "Mr. Baby Proofer," a thirty-minute video that shows parents how to create a safe environment.

❄ Ask for advice at any of the baby super stores. A salesperson will talk you through what you need in order to create a safe home.

❄ Hire a baby proofing expert. Howard Applebaum of Babyproofers Plus (800-880-2191) will come to your home for a free consultation, determine what you need, prepare an estimate, and install everything. We both used Howard, who gives seminars on child safety at local hospitals, and we highly recommend him. Another baby proofing company is Child-Safe Homes, Inc. (718-433-1446), run by Richard Pucciarelli, who also provides a free consultation, price estimate, and installation. It will cost $250 to $400 to baby proof a two-bedroom apartment in New York.

Many people baby proof their own apartments. Howard Applebaum suggests the following safety tips:

Poisons or toxic materials should not be stored under the sink; place them high up out of your baby's reach.

✳ Attach all busy boxes, mirrors, or crib toys on the wall side of the crib, so that your baby cannot use the objects to climb out of the crib. Do not mount a wall hanging above the crib, where your child can pull it down and perhaps dislodge nails.

✳ Toilet lids should be locked closed.

✳ Keep all trash containers locked up and out of baby's way.

✳ Remove tall lamps or coatracks or block them with furniture, so that your baby can't pull them over.

✳ When cooking, all pot handles should be turned inward so your baby cannot reach them. Use back burners when possible.

✳ Separate plants and babies. Some plants are poisonous, and a young child may eat the leaves or pull the whole plant on top of himself.

✳ Hanging cords from answering machines, phones, lamps, and appliances should be out of your baby's reach.

✳ Do not take pills or medication in front of children; they mimic what they see.

✳ Remove all soaps, razors, and shampoos from around the edge of the bathtub.

✳ Do not use tacks or staples to secure electrical cords to walls; they can fall out or be pulled out and swallowed. Use tape.

✳ Discard plastic dry cleaner bags before entering the house. Babies can suffocate in them or pull off pieces and choke on them.

✳ Keep emergency phone numbers, including poison control center, near all telephones.

✳ To prevent carpeting from sliding, use a foam grid padding beneath it.

✳ Babies like to pull off the tips from doorstops. Place some glue inside the cap, then stick the cap back onto the doorstop.

✳ Remove magnets from your refrigerator door. If they fall to the floor and break, a child may pick up the pieces and swallow them. Invest in baby magnets or plastic non-breakable ones.

✳ If you have a fireplace, place a piece of carpet or foam on the whole base so your child won't bang into the brick.

✳ Get a bathtub spout cover to prevent your child from hitting his head against it.

✳ If you have a home gym, keep that room

closed when you're not in it. Babies can get their fingers stuck in the spokes of exercise bikes, put their fingers in the gears, or pull weights onto themselves.

✳ Glass panels in coffee tables can break under the weight of a child. Replace with acrylic.

✳ Mobiles should be removed when a child is five to seven months old. A baby of that age can pull the mobile down, or be injured if the little strings from the mobile can be wrapped around his fingers.

✳ Cords for window blinds should be lifted high and out of reach. Babies can accidentally wrap them around themselves.

✳ Wash out cleaning fluid bottles before putting them in your recycling bin. Just a drop of cleaning fluid can cause serious injury to a baby.

✳ Never leave an infant alone in the bath tub. Ignore telephone calls and doorbells. Babies can drown in just an inch of water. Never leave a tub with water standing in it.

✳ Check the underside of upholstered furniture for loose staples or sharp points.

10 · baby and toddler clothing

If you've always thought baby clothes were the cutest things in the world, here's your chance to have some of your very own. New York stores have all the baby clothing you need, want, or can dream of from discounted sleepers for less than $5 to custom-made dresses for $400. There's tons of adorable stuff to choose from, but don't bring all of it home at once. Babies grow very, very quickly, and the outfit that fit the last time you put it on may not even come close a week later. We'll tell you about some of the best clothing shops in the city to help you save time, energy, and money.

SHOPPING TIPS

If your gifts include too many outfits in three- and six-month sizes, return most of them for a credit, or exchange them for twelve- or eighteen-month sizes. Don't dawdle, either. If you put it off, you'll find them in the closet, unworn, a year later.

✳ Pay attention to a store's return policy. Most of the shops—especially the European-style boutiques, such as Jacadi and Au Chat Botte —are strict. Department stores tend to be the most lenient; goods can usually be brought back for cash or credit for up to one year.

✳ Ask about sales. Small shops often have

January and June/July special pricing events; some have quarterly sales. Department stores always seem to have sales. In some shops, you won't be able to use gift certificates on sale items.

✳ If you plan to shop with your little one in tow, use a baby carrier or small stroller. Some of these stores are small, crowded, and you may have to walk up a flight of stairs.

✳ Onesie outfits are practical. You can't have too many of these pullover, short sleeve T-shirts with bottom snaps, to layer under winter clothes or use as-is in hot weather. All the stores carry onesies, in a variety of price ranges. Buy the least expensive, 100 percent cotton ones you can find.

✳ Think cotton. It's cozy, soft, and easily washable. (Your pediatrician will probably tell you to wash your baby's clothes for the first year in the non-detergents Dreft or Ivory Snow, which do not irritate a baby's sensitive skin.)

✳ You'll find it convenient to have many sleeping outfits, but test several before buying a bunch to see which your baby prefers. Pamela bought half a dozen Carter's sleeping gowns with drawstring bottoms, but found out that Rebecca was uncomfortable with her feet restricted. She exchanged them for open

Top Seven Things to Know About Baby Clothes

1. Buy your layette, but wait to buy more clothes until all the gifts are in; you might not need as much as you think.

2. All clothes should be machine washable.

3. If you receive many gifts in small sizes, always exchange some for larger ones.

4. Use clothing with snaps around the bottom for easy changing.

5. Buy ahead when possible; winter coats, for example, are on sale in January.

6. Try to borrow expensive items like snowsuits and coats.

7. Patronize stores with liberal return policies.

sleeper bag pajamas, and Rebecca was much happier. (All sleepwear must be 100 percent polyester to be flame retardant.)

✳ Don't buy any infant clothes with strings around or near the neck, which can be dangerous. Most manufacturers today have stopped making baby clothes with strings.

✳ Give some thought to how and when you'll do laundry. Your baby is going to go through several different outfits a day. If you have a washer and dryer in your apartment, and it's easy to throw in a load at odd moments, a large layette may be unnecessary. If you use a machine in your building's basement or take clothing to a neighborhood laundromat, it may be more convenient and easier on your pocketbook to stock up a relatively large supply of clothing.

✳ Many stores have prepared an essential layette list for you. Take such lists with a grain of salt, keeping in mind your own budget and storage space.

Here's a practical layette:

FOR BABY

6 onesies

2 side-snap or side-tie shirts
    (until umbilical cord separates)

6 stretchies or coveralls, which cover your
    baby from neck to feet, and have snaps

4 kimonos, sleep gowns, or sleeper bags

2 caps

6 pairs of socks

1 snowsuit (for winter babies)

4 receiving blankets (to lay the baby down
    on and wrap her up in)

2 heavier blankets (one for stroller,
    one for crib)

3 hooded towel/washcloth sets

12 cloth diapers (for burping the baby,
    laying her down on)

4 bibs

1 outdoor hat (keeps winter babies warm,
    protects summer babies from sun)

1 pair cotton mittens (to prevent your baby
    from scratching her face)

1 pair outdoor mittens (for winter babies)

baby scissors, nail clipper, non-glass
    thermometer, nasal aspirator,
    hairbrush/comb

bath tub/bath sponge

FOR CRIB

2 quilted mattress pads

2 waterproof liners

4 fitted crib sheets

6 crib bibs (to protect sheets from
    baby spit up)

1 bumper pad

THE STORES

Au Chat Botte

1192 Madison Avenue at 87th Street

722-6474

Hours: Monday through Saturday 10 A.M. to 5:30 P.M.; Closed Sunday.

Return Policy: Store credit only.

This small, pretty French boutique carries beautiful imported baby clothing and accessories. It's for truly special gifts.

Baby Guess

775 Madison Avenue at 66th Street

628-2229

Hours: Monday through Saturday 10 A.M. to 6 P.M.; Closed Sunday.

Return Policy: Store credit only.

Baby Guess features 100 percent cotton clothing for children from three months to six years old. You'll find an extensive selection of jeans, overalls, and shorts. All clothing has the Baby Guess label, and prices are moderate.

Bambini

1367 Third Avenue at 78th Street 717-6742

Hours: Monday through Saturday 10 A.M. to 7 P.M.; Sunday 12 P.M. to 6 P.M.

Return Policy: Store credit within seven days.

A very Upper East Side shop, Bambini offers fine Italian clothing for children from three months to eight years old. Their selection is dressy, formal, and pricey; this is a good place to purchase a holiday or special occasion outfit for a boy or girl.

Barney's

660 Madison Avenue at 61st Street

826-8900

Hours: Monday through Friday 10 A.M. to 8 P.M.; Saturday 10 A.M. to 7 P.M.; Sunday 12 P.M. to 6 P.M.

Return Policy: Refund with receipt.

The children's department at Barney's is small but well-stocked with brands such as Grain de Luna, Haute for Tots, Tapemeasure, Suddenly Mommies, Baby Armadillo, Erin's Babies, Metropolitan Prairie, and Barney's private label. Just as you'd expect, most of the clothes and accessories—for newborns to children age four—are stylish and expensive. The department also carries pretty towels and washcloths, shoes, baby albums, hand-painted pillows, and stuffed animals.

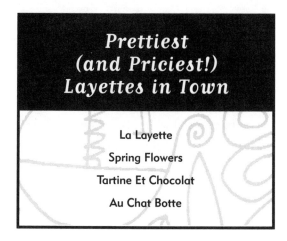

Prettiest (and Priciest!) Layettes in Town

La Layette

Spring Flowers

Tartine Et Chocolat

Au Chat Botte

Bloomingdale's*

1000 Third Avenue at 59th Street 705-2000

Hours: Monday through Friday 10 A.M. to 8:30 P.M.; Saturday 10 A.M. to 7 P.M.; Sunday 11 A.M. to 7 P.M.

Return Policy: Lenient.

The sprawling children's department on Bloomingdale's eighth floor has one section for layettes, newborns, and toddlers, then separate sections for girls, boys, and teens. Bloomingdale's carries a wide variety of brands: Carter's, Little Me, Baby Dior, Classic Pooh, Mini Clasix, Absorba, Ralph Lauren Baby, Esprit, Flapdoodles, Baby B'Gosh, Baby Guess, and their private label, Next Generation. You'll also find many accessories, toys, and gifts; and great end of season sales.

Bombalulus

332 Columbus Avenue at 75th Street

501-8248

Hours: Monday through Wednesday 12 P.M. to 8 P.M.; Thursday through Saturday 12 P.M. to 8 P.M.; Sunday 11 A.M. to 8 P.M.

Return Policy: Store credit only.

This tiny store is a nice addition to Columbus Avenue. The store's name is African, and loosely translates to "a group of artists working together." Most of the clothes are handmade and moderately priced. You'll find hand-painted onesies, T-shirts, shorts, leggings, sweatshirts, and hand-sewn jackets and hats. The store imports colorful clothing from Bali and Guatemala, as well as some unique toys.

Bonpoint

1269 Madison Avenue at 90th Street

722-7720

811 Madison Avenue at 68th Street

879-0900

Hours: Monday through Saturday 10 A.M. to 6 P.M.; Closed Sunday.

Return Policy: Store credit only. No returns on sale items.

All clothes have the Bonpoint label and are imported from Paris. Sizes begin at three months and go up to size 16 for girls, size 12 or 14 for boys. The store has a wide selection and is easy to shop in, but prices can be on the high side. The atmosphere is formal, but if you (or Grandma) are looking for only the best, the beautifully tailored French clothing is perfect for special occasions.

Bunnies

100-102 Delancey Street at Ludlow Street
529-7567
Hours: Monday through Sunday 9 A.M. to 7 P.M.
Return Policy: Refund with receipt within ten days, otherwise store credit only.

Bunnies is a discount children's department store. While they carry baby furniture and equipment, their selection of clothing—mostly moderately priced casual play clothes—is their strong suit.

Catimini

1284 Madison Avenue at 91st Street
987-0688
Hours: Monday through Saturday 10 A.M. to 7 P.M.; Sunday 12 P.M. to 5 P.M.

Summer Hours: Monday through Saturday 10 A.M. to 6 P.M.; Closed Sunday.
Return Policy: Store credit only. Sale items cannot be returned.

Catimini's stylish French clothing is unique. Mostly casual play clothes; sizes range from newborn to age fourteen. (Catimini's own label is also carried by Saks Fifth Avenue and Small Change.)

Century 21

22 Cortlandt Street, World Trade Center
227-9092
Hours: Monday through Wednesday 7:45 A.M. to 7 P.M.; Thursday 7:45 A.M. to 8:30 P.M.; Friday 7:45 A.M. to 8 P.M.; Saturday 10 A.M. to 7 P.M.
Return Policy: Refund with a receipt, otherwise store credit only.

Century 21, the discount department store, has a large children's department with brands like Carter's, Little Me, Baby Dior, Gerber, and Absorba. It's not difficult to find a bargain, with prices hovering around twenty-five percent below retail. Accessories include diaper bags, cloth diapers, bibs, and more. It's crowded, especially on weekends; it's best to shop here without your baby.

The Children's Place*

901 Avenue of the Americas at 32nd Street,

The Manhattan Mall 268-7696

173 East 86th Street 831-5100

Hours: Monday through Saturday 10 A.M. to 8 P.M.; Sunday 11 A.M. to 6 P.M.

Return Policy: No sale is ever final.

The Children's Place (a chain with shops in many New Jersey malls) is a real find, and it could well be the next Gap. The store is clean, its return policy is flexible, and the clothing is comfortable, of high quality, stylish, and affordable. The collections come in bright and traditional colors and are basic, with some fashion sense. We saw beautiful fall/winter corduroys in rich, royal colors—deep blue, ruby red, and emerald green.

Chock's

74 Orchard Street 473-1929

Hours: Sunday through Thursday 9 A.M. to 5 P.M.; Friday 9 A.M. to 1:30 P.M.; Closed Saturday.

Return Policy: Refund with receipt within thirty days.

Chock's has been in business since 1921. This small discount store on the Lower East Side has layette items by Carter's, Gerber, and Sara's Prints; waterproof crib sheets by Snug'n Dry; and toilet-training kits. Most of the gifts are wooden toys—blocks, trains, and cars.

The Chocolate Soup

946 Madison Avenue at 74th Street

861-2210

Hours: Monday through Saturday 10 A.M. to 6 P.M.; Sunday 1 P.M. to 6 P.M. (September through December only).

Return Policy: Store credit within two weeks.

This tiny store is worth a special trip. They hand-dye much of their clothing, and you'll find colors you won't find elsewhere. Oshkosh B'Gosh overalls, for example, are available in a dozen colors, as are moderately priced Flap-doodles T-shirts and leggings. Other brands include Jean Bourget, Petit Boy, Joseph Baby, Pappa & Ciccio, and Tapemeasure. Sizes run from newborn to age twelve or fourteen. Especially attractive is their wonderful selection of handmade toys—wooden animals, country dolls, doll house furniture, and puppets.

Coco & Z*

222 Columbus Avenue at 70th Street

721-0415

Hours: Monday through Friday 10 A.M.

to 7 P.M.; Saturday 11 A.M. to 7 P.M.; Sunday 12 P.M. to 6 P.M.

Return Policy: Store credit only.

A relative newcomer to the Columbus Avenue baby scene, Coco & Z is a valued neighborhood addition. Opened by two Upper West Side parents (whose children's nicknames are Coco and Z), this store features moderately priced play clothes. If you think stylish boys' clothes are hard to find, this is the place to shop. The selection for boys as well as girls is excellent, in sizes from newborn (layette) to ten years. Brands include Milena, Baby Armadillo, Rebel Kids, and Metropolitan Prairie. Coco & Z also sells wonderful gift baskets for newborns or toddlers.

Daffy's

111 Fifth Avenue at 18th Street 529-4477

335 Madison Avenue at 44th Street
557-4422

135 East 57th Street at Lexington Avenue
376-4477

1311 Broadway 736-4477

Hours: Open seven days a week; hours vary at each location. Call ahead.

Return Policy: Refund within fourteen days, otherwise store credit only.

Funkiest Kids' Clothes

Space Kiddets

Z'Baby Company

Peanut Butter and Jane

Daffy's is a discount store for the whole family. Their children's department is particularly good, and our downtown friends swear by Daffy's for some of the best bargains in town. It's sort of like Loehmann's, so be prepared to pick through racks and hunt for infant clothes that were misplaced in the toddler section. Brands include Peter Rabbit, Buster Brown, Mini Basix, Absorba, and Flapdoodles. Pamela picked up Flapdoodle leggings here for Rebecca for $5.99.

Baby Gap*

Locations throughout the city.

Hours: Monday through Friday 9:30 A.M. to 7:30 P.M.; Saturday 9:30 A.M. to 7 P.M.; Sunday 12 P.M. to 5 P.M.

Return Policy: Lenient.

Who doesn't know and love the Gap? There are now at least ten Baby Gap stores in town, usually within grownup Gap stores. The Gap's baby clothing, often in 100 percent cotton, comes in traditional colors and styles. Nothing outrageous here, just good old-fashioned T-shirts, sweaters, leggings, and socks that you would wear yourself—and the sales are great! Play clothes are comfortable and hold up well after repeated washings. Just be prepared to see most of the other babies at playgroup wearing the exact same thing.

Greenstones Et Cie

442 Columbus Avenue at 81st Street
580-4322

Greenstones, Too

1184 Madison Avenue at 86th Street
427-1665

Hours: Open Monday through Saturday; Sunday on Columbus only. Call for hours.
Return Policy: Store credit only. No returns on sale items.

These family-owned-and-operated stores contain a wide selection of clothing for children from newborn to age ten for girls, age fourteen for boys. Some brands featured include I.K.K.S., Jean Bourget, Gallipette, and Petit Boy. Prices are moderate for sportswear and more expensive for dressier designer items.

Gymboree

1120 Madison Avenue at 83rd Street
717-6702
1132 Third Avenue at 76th Street 517-5548
2015 Broadway at 69th Street 595-7662
Hours: Monday through Friday 10 A.M. to 7 P.M.; Saturday 10 A.M. to 6 P.M.; Sunday 11 A.M. to 5 P.M.
Return Policy: Lenient.

The large, roomy Gymboree stores (a handful in New York, more in outlying suburbs, and across the country) specialize in play clothes and active wear for boys and girls from newborn to eight years. The moderately priced clothes are 100 percent cotton and come in brightly colored patterns and designs. New collections arrive every six to eight weeks.

Jacadi

1281 Madison Avenue at 91st Street
369-1616
787 Madison Avenue at 67th Street
535-3200
Hours: Monday through Saturday 10 A.M. to 6 P.M.; Thursday 10 A.M. to 7 P.M.; Sunday 12 P.M. to 5 P.M.
Return Policy: Store credit only. No returns on

sale items.

The two Jacadi stores in New York (more in outlying suburbs) are independently owned and operated. The merchandise is imported form France and is mostly the Jacadi label. Available are both play and dressy clothes for newborns to twelve-year-olds, as well as towels, nursery furniture, and wallpaper. Be discriminating about what you buy, because returns are next to impossible. Watch for the June and January sales.

Judy's Fancies

249 East 45th Street 681-8115

Hours: Tuesday through Friday 10:30 A.M. to 6:30 P.M.; Saturday 11 A.M. to 5:30 P.M.; Closed Sunday and Monday.

Return Policy: Exchange, or refund if customer truly doesn't like the work.

Judith Correa recently opened this tiny storefront where she handsews clothing for newborns to toddlers (and creates beautifully tailored christening gowns for $85 and up). Other prices range from $28 for a simple cotton dress, to $45 for a velvet outfit. Her clothing is pastel-colored and very European in style. She will custom-make clothes for children of all ages and sizes.

Julian & Sara

103 Mercer Street 226-1989

Hours: Tuesday through Friday 11:30 A.M. to 7 P.M.; Saturday and Sunday 12 P.M. to 6 P.M.; Closed Monday.

Return Policy: Store credit with receipt. No returns on sale items.

This tiny boutique imports most of its clothing from Europe and carries an especially good selection for girls, with everything from party dresses to play clothes. Brands include Jean Bourget and I.K.K.S. Julian & Sara also carries shoes and accessories.

Kids Are Magic*

2293 Broadway at 83rd Street 875-9240

Hours: Monday through Wednesday 10 A.M. to 7:45 P.M.; Thursday through Saturday 10 A.M. to 8:45 P.M.; Sunday 10 A.M. to 6 P.M.

Return Policy: Refund with receipt within twelve days. No returns on sale items.

Kids Are Magic is probably the best discount children's store in New York. The selection changes, but you'll often find names like Mini Basix, Tumble Togs, Carter's, Agabang, Day Kids, Flaphappy, Levi's, Weebox, Baby Guess, Lee, and Miniwaves. Sort through the selection of play clothes, swimsuits, and accessories in sizes newborn to 4T, and you'll find incredibly low prices on onesies, T-shirts, and pajamas. Upstairs is a toy department that carries Fisher-Price, Little Tikes, stuffed animals, puzzles, and games. The store has the best prices on Pampers on the Upper West Side.

Kids Row

1626 First Avenue at 85th Street 327-1063
Hours: Monday through Friday 10 A.M. to 7 P.M.; Saturday and Sunday 11 A.M. to 5 P.M.
Return Policy: Store credit only.

This children's boutique features a variety of handmade American clothes, most of which have the Kids Row label. Kids Row carries more girls' clothing than boys' but has a nice selection of unisex accessories.

Kids "R" Us

1293 Broadway at 34th Street 643-0714
Hours: Monday and Friday 9 A.M. to 9 P.M.; Tuesday, Wednesday, and Saturday 9 A.M. to 8 P.M.; Thursday 9 A.M. to 9:30 P.M.; Sunday 11 A.M. to 7 P.M.
Return Policy: Lenient.

This huge store located next to the Manhattan Mall has it all for newborns to boy's size 20 and girl's size 14. The store is as full as it can be, but well laid out, and organized by size and gender. Everything here is discounted—Carter's stretchies (our benchmark) were priced at two for $14, the lowest price we saw. Other brands sold here include Global Kids, Healthtex, Levi's, Oshkosh B'Gosh, Koala Kids, Jet Set, Mickey & Co., Jordache, Color & Co., Baby Beluga, Classic Pooh, and Stix 'n' Stone. Kids "R" Us also has a nice selection of toys, books, and stuffed animals, as well as accessories such as socks, barrettes, and knapsacks.

Koh's Kids

311 Greenwich Street at Chambers Street 791-6915
Hours: Monday through Saturday 11 A.M. to 7 P.M.; Sunday 11 A.M. to 5 P.M..
Return Policy: Store credit only.

This very small store offers funky, quality children's clothing (newborn to seven years old). Koh's Kids clothing ranges from dressy to casual, from dresses ($20 to $70) to T-shirts ($12 to $25). Brands include Baby Armadillo and Cary. You'll also find cute toys and accessories.

Kreinen's

301 Grand Street at Allen Street 925-0239

*Hours: Monday through Friday and
Sunday 9 A.M. to 5 P.M.; Closed Saturday.*

Return Policy: Refund with receipt.

This Lower East Side shop has a good
selection of layette items from Little Me, Baby
Dior, Carter's, Quiltex, and Sara's Prints, plus
everyday play clothes, outerwear, and sleepwear. Its more spacious setting makes it the
easiest of the neighborhood children's stores
to shop.

La Layette . . . Et Plus Ltd.*

170 East 61st Street 688-7072

*Hours: Monday through Saturday 11 A.M.
to 6 P.M.; Closed Sunday; Closed Saturdays
in the summer.*

Return Policy: Store credit only.

This tiny boutique near Bloomingdale's
specializes in personalized service (an
appointment is recommended) and layettes.
Most everything is made especially for La
Layette, and the selection is absolutely gorgeous. As expected, these complete layettes
are rather expensive: from $500 to $5,000,
with an average price of $800. Come see
their beautiful (many one-of-a-kind) bris and

christening outfits and custom clothing for
older children (like a girl's party dress for
$350). Hand-painted cribs ($800) are sold
with coordinating sheets, bumpers, and pillows. Everything is exquisite!

Lester's*

1522 Second Avenue at 79th Street
734-9292

*Hours: Monday, Tuesday, Wednesday,
and Friday 10 A.M. to 7 P.M.; Thursday 10 A.M.
to 8 P.M.; Saturday 10 A.M. to 6 P.M.; Sunday
12 P.M. to 5 P.M.*

Return Policy: Refund with receipt within
seven days, otherwise store credit only.

This discount store has a wide variety of
play clothes, accessories, and shoes for newborns to children ages six to eight. You can
find Carter's, Little Me, Mini Basix, I.K.K.S,
Jean Bourget, Mini Man, Flapdoodles, and
My Boy Sam. Much of the merchandise is
priced below their competitors, making this
a definite find on the Upper East Side.

Little Folks

123 East 23rd Street 982-9669

*Hours: Monday through Thursday
9:30 A.M. to 7 P.M.; Friday 9:30 to before*

sundown (call ahead); Sunday 12 P.M. to
5 P.M.; Closed Saturday.
Return Policy: Refund with receipt within
seven days, otherwise store credit only.

Little Folks could fit in the super store category, since it carries cribs, highchairs, and
accessories, but we call it a clothing store
because the large, discounted selection is
terrific. Pamela bought Rebecca's snowsuit
at Little Folks for $40 less than she saw it
at another store. Brands include Brambilla,
Carter's, Absorba, Weebok, and Sara's Prints.

Little Senli
30 Rockefeller Plaza 582-1083
Hours: Monday through Friday 9:30 A.M.
to 6 P.M.; Saturday 9:30 A.M. to 6:30 P.M.;
Sunday 10 A.M. to 5 P.M.
Return Policy: Store credit only.

There's lovely clothing for newborns as
well as gifts such as beautifully packaged
layette sets and baskets, dish sets and stuffed
animals. The accessories—hair bows and the
like—are especially cute.

Lolli Pop
241 Third Avenue at 19th Street 995-0977
Hours: Monday through Friday 11 A.M. to

Best Places for Sale Items Under $10

Gap

Talbot's Kids

Kids Are Magic

7 P.M.; Saturday and Sunday 12 P.M. to 6 P.M.
Return Policy: Store credit only.

Lolli Pop is a great resource in an area
of the city with few baby stores. Most of the
clothes here are European imports: Cacharel,
Arthur Confiture, and Prive de Dessert. Lolli
Pop also creates gift baskets.

Lord & Taylor
424 Fifth Avenue at 35th Street
391-3344, ext. 3934
Hours: Monday and Tuesday 10 A.M. to
7 P.M.; Wednesday, Thursday, and Friday
10 A.M. to 8:30 P.M.; Saturday 10 A.M. to
7 P.M.; Sunday 11 A.M. to 6 P.M.
Return Policy: Lenient.

Spacious and inviting, the children's
department at this grand old department
store is filled with a wide variety of quality

layette items and clothing of many brands, including the attractive Lord & Taylor private label. There's also a wonderful selection of stuffed animals, diaper bags, knapsacks, bedding sets, and christening outfits.

Macy's

Herald Square, 151 West 34th Street

695-4400

Hours: Monday, Thursday, and Friday 10 A.M. to 8:30 P.M.; Tuesday, Wednesday, and Saturday 10 A.M. to 7 P.M.; Sunday 11 A.M. to 7 P.M.

Return Policy: Lenient.

The children's department sells everything from clothing to Stride Rite shoes, and offers a changing room for your baby. Macy's carries many brands for newborns and older, and devotes an entire area to Oshkosh B'Gosh, Disney, and Mickey & Co. The prices are generally moderate, and you can always find something on sale.

Madison Avenue Maternity & Baby

1043 Madison Avenue at 80th Street

988-8686

Hours: Monday through Friday 10 A.M. to 7 P.M.; Saturday 10 A.M. to 6 P.M.; Sunday 12 P.M. to 5 P.M.

Return Policy: Store credit only.

This is a good place to find unique baby clothing. Baby Graziella, Arthur Confiture, and Grain de Lune, among others, are featured for ages newborn to twelve months. The store also has a small selection of books, diaper bags, and other miscellaneous accessories.

Magic Windows*

1186 Madison Avenue at 87th Street

289-0028

Hours: Monday through Friday 10 A.M. to 6 P.M.; Thursday 9 A.M. to 7 P.M.; Sunday 12 P.M. to 5 P.M.; Closed Sunday in July and August.

Return Policy: Store credit only. No returns on sale items.

Magic Windows carries a nifty layette assortment, including Petit Bateau, Absorba, Carter's, and Little Me, and other children's clothing from Florence Eisman, Vive La Fete, L'Agneau D'Or, and Anna Vini. This is also the place to find baby clothes with hand-made smocking. Magic Windows carries Periwinkle cribs, changing tables, and bureaus.

Monkeys and Bears

506 Amsterdam Avenue at 84th Street
873-2673
Hours: Monday through Friday 11 A.M. to 7 P.M.; Saturday 11 A.M. to 6 P.M.; Sunday 12 P.M. to 6 P.M. Closed Sunday in the summer.
Return Policy: Store credit only.

This small shop has clothing for newborns to two-year-olds and a wide range of accessories, gift items, and custom bedding and linen. Clothing brands sold here include Lori Lyn, Flapdoodles, Petit Bateau, and My Boy Sam. Monkeys and Bears gets crowded easily, so bring your baby in a baby carrier rather than a stroller. Prices range from moderate to expensive.

Morris Brothers

2322 Broadway at 84th Street 724-9000
Hours: Monday through Saturday 9:30 A.M. to 6:30 P.M.; Sunday 12 P.M. to 5:30 P.M.
Return Policy: Store credit only. No returns on sale items.

Morris Brothers is an Upper West Side landmark. For thirty-five years New Yorkers have shopped here for newborn and toddler clothing as well as apparel for teens and adults. (And it's an official camp outfitter; this happens sooner than you'd think.) Most clothes are casual and moderately priced, with brands including Sophie Dess, Deux par Deux, Zutano, City Lights, Carter's, Absorba, Flapdoodles, and Oshkosh B'Gosh. The sales staff is helpful and knowledgeable.

New York Exchange for Woman's Work

1095 Third Avenue at 64th Street 753-2330
Hours: Monday through Saturday 10 A.M. to 6 P.M.; Closed Sunday.
Return Policy: Store credit only within two weeks.

For over 100 years the Exchange has been a treasure trove of beautiful handmade articles. You will find beautiful one-of-a-kind baby blankets, dresses with hand-smocking, baby booties, onesies, and more. Prices range from moderate to expensive.

O'givee

Manhattan Mall (4th Floor)

901 Sixth Avenue at 32nd Street 947-1667

Hours: Monday through Saturday 10 A.M.
to 8 P.M.; Sunday 11 A.M. to 6 P.M.

Return Policy: Store credit only.

Part souvenir/accessory shop, part clothing store, O'givee is worth a look if you're on your way to the Manhattan Mall. Clothing is mostly casual and trendy, with brands such as Miniwaves, Baby Guess, Isabella, Harlequin, and Mullin Square. They carry many "character" items, especially from Disney, and a large selection of children's accessories.

Oilily

870 Madison Avenue at 70th Street
628-0100

Hours: Monday through Saturday 10 A.M.
to 6 P.M.; Sunday 12 P.M. to 5 P.M.

Return Policy: Refund with receipt within two weeks, otherwise store credit only.

Carrying exclusively their own designs, this Dutch store's trademark is bright colors and unique patterns. Children's sizes start at three months. They sell sportswear, play clothes, and shoes. You'll find that the prices are comparable to other Madison Avenue European clothing stores.

Old Navy Clothing Co.*

610 Sixth Avenue at 18th Street 645-0663

Hours: Monday through Saturday
9:30 A.M. to 9 P.M.; Sunday 11 A.M. to 7 P.M.

Return Policy: Refund with receipt within thirty days.

This is a great warehouse-like store to visit, even if you don't need kiddy clothes. It has its own café (with quite a few strollers parked next to the tables) and sells lots of candy, gadgets, candles, and lotions, plus basic jeans and other essentials for grownups. Upstairs, you will find reasonably priced, 100 percent cotton items for newborns and older. The Old Navy Clothing Co. is owned by the Gap and is a lower-priced alternative. There are adorable infant dresses for $10, bibs for $3, and onesies in bright colors for $5.50. Be warned: Old Navy is packed on weekends.

Oshkosh B'Gosh Store

586 Fifth Avenue at 47th Street 827-0098

Hours: Monday through Saturday 10 A.M.
to 7 P.M.; Sunday 12 P.M. to 5 P.M.

Return Policy: Refund with receipt, otherwise store credit only.

This big, bright store is neatly organized by collection, and by child's age and sex. The clothes (from newborn to 6X) are colorful, 100 percent cotton, and reasonably priced.

Peanut Butter & Jane*

617 Hudson Street at 12th Street 620-7952
*Hours: Monday through Saturday
10:30 A.M. to 7 P.M.; Sunday 12 P.M. to 6 P.M.*
Return Policy: Store credit only.

This attractively cluttered shop is filled to the brim with all types of clothing and shoes, from everyday to funky or dressy. Prices are reasonable, with T-shirts for $12 and up, dresses for $50 and up, and rompers/onesies for $25 and up. Popular brands here include Earthlings, Petals, and City Lights. There is a small play area with books and toys.

Prince & Princess

33 East 68th Street 879-8989
*Hours: Monday through Saturday 10 A.M.
to 6 P.M.; Closed Sunday.*
Return Policy: Store credit only.

With prices such as $185 for a knit one-sie, this European children's boutique is truly for princes and princesses. It may be just the place to find a special holiday suit or dress.

The store carries clothing for newborns to children age twelve, but will take special orders for women up to age twenty. Be prepared to browse on your own.

Regine's Kids

2688 Broadway at 102nd Street 864-8705
*Hours: Monday through Saturday
9:30 A.M. to 8 P.M.; Sunday 11 A.M. to 6 P.M.*
Return Policy: Refund with receipt within seven days.

Uptown moms swear by Regine's Kids as the only place in their neighborhood to pick up baby supplies and quality clothing. The store carries layette clothing as well as brands such as Flapdoodles, Oshkosh and Levi's from newborn to size 14. It also sells furniture and accessories for babies.

Robin's Nest

1168 Lexington Avenue at 80th Street
737-2004
*Hours: Monday through Saturday 11 A.M. to
6 P.M.; Closed Sunday; Call for summer hours.*
Return Policy: Store credit only. No returns on sale items.

Robin's Nest is tiny, but well stocked with clothes for newborns to children up to age

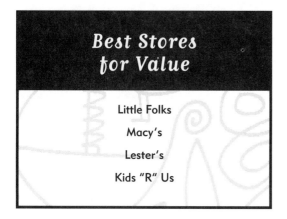

Best Stores for Value

Little Folks
Macy's
Lester's
Kids "R" Us

excellent infant and toddler department and carries a wide range of brands, plus a number of designers not found elsewhere. The department is wonderfully laid out and easy to shop. For the layette there is Absorba, Nathan, and Simonetta; for toddlers, there is Sara's Prints, Heartstrings Baby, Florence Eisenman, Sylvia Whyte, Galipette, Baby Lulu, Monkey Wear, Catamini, and more.

twelve. Most styles are casual, and brands include Miniature, Best T-shirts, Hank Player, Jean Bourget, Galipette, Kid Basics, Lori Lyn, and L'Agneau D'Or. The store also carries accessories, such as suspenders, barrettes, bibs, hats, and socks. Prices range from moderate for T-shirts to expensive for a large selection of sweaters, including one with an American flag for $82.

Saks Fifth Avenue*

611 Fifth Avenue at 50th Street 753-4000
Hours: Monday, Tuesday, Wednesday, Friday, and Saturday 10 A.M. to 7 P.M.; Thursday 10 A.M. to 8 P.M.; Sunday 12 P.M. to 6 P.M.
Return Policy: Lenient.

This top-notch department store has an

Small Change

964 Lexington Avenue at 70th Street
772-6455
Hours: Monday through Saturday 10 A.M. to 5 P.M.; Closed Sunday; Closed Saturday in July and August.
Return Policy: Store credit only.

This small store, with clothing on the expensive side, has many loyal fans. Small Change has clothing for newborns up to size 14, but no layette department. The mostly European brands include Jean Bourget, Mini Man, L'Agneau D'Or, New Man, Magil, Petit Boy, Kelsy, Petit Bateau, Deux par Deux, Françoise Bouthiller, and Giesswein. You'll also find an outstanding selection of snowsuits, jackets, raincoats, and hats.

Space Kiddets*

46 East 21st Street 420-9878

Hours: Monday, Tuesday, and Friday: 10:30 A.M. to 6 P.M.; Wednesday and Thursday 10:30 A.M. to 7 P.M.; Saturday 10:30 A.M. to 5:30 P.M.; Closed Sunday.

Return Policy: Store credit only.

Most of the clothing here is funky, but moderately priced. Brands include Maxou, Mouse Feathers, Mini Thallion, and I.K.K.S. Space Kiddets has a little of everything, including toys, table and chair sets, fantasy play clothes, even Elvis memorabilia!

Spring Flowers*

1050 Third Avenue at 62nd Street

758-2669

905 Madison Avenue at 72nd Street

717-8182

410 Columbus Avenue at 78th Street

721-2337

Hours: Open every day; closed Sunday in July. Call for hours.

Return Policy: Store credit only.

Spring Flowers is known for its extensive collection of top-quality French and Italian clothes for children, newborn to ten years. (A Spring Flowers Layette store adjoins the Third Avenue Store.) Spring Flowers carries play clothes and an outstanding selection of party and holiday clothes for boys and girls. Dresses are sold with matching hats, tights, purses, and accessories. Boys' navy blazers and flannel pants are beautifully tailored. Designers carried here include Sophie Dess, Florian, Petit Bateau, Giesswien, Cacharel, Joan Calabrese, Pappa & Ciccia, Françoise Bouthillier, and Sarah Louise. Spring Flowers also has a wide selection of European shoes, including the Sonnet brand from England— popular first walkers. Prices are high, as you'd expect, and the service is excellent.

Talbot's Kids & Babies*

1523 Second Avenue at 79th Street

570-1630

Hours: Monday, Tuesday, Wednesday, Friday, and Saturday 9:30 A.M. to 7 P.M.; Thursday 9:30 A.M. to 8 P.M.; Sunday 12 P.M. to 5 P.M.

Return Policy: Refund with receipt, otherwise, store credit only.

This large, well-lit store sells attractive clothes for newborns to size 16 for boys and girls. Their high-quality, preppy style of clothing is worth a look. The store concentrates on toddlers and older children; the layette and infant/

toddler section is smaller. They have excellent sales, with prices often half the original.

Tartine Et Chocolat

746 Madison Avenue at 64th Street
744-0975
Hours: Monday through Saturday 10 A.M. to 6 P.M.; Closed Sunday
Return Policy: Store credit only. No returns on sale items.

This European boutique features a large, gorgeous layette selection, with onesies from $50 to sleepers for $80. Dressy children's clothing, made under the store's own label, is truly special. Sizes range from 0 (preemie baby) to children age twelve. The store also carries strollers, bassinets, car seats, sassy seats, wallpaper, luggage, fragrance, and many gift items.

Tutti Bambini

1490 First Avenue at 76th Street 472-4238
Hours: Monday through Friday 11 A.M. to 7 P.M.; Saturday 11 A.M. to 6 P.M.; Closed Sunday.
Return Policy: Store credit only. No returns on sale items.

Tutti Bambini is a small boutique that carries a full line of clothing and accessories for newborns to pre-teens. Brands include Erin's Baby, Mini Man, Hank Player, Lori Lyn, Catimini, Galipette, and Annie's Antics. You'll also find some sumptuous (and expensive) Ruth Hornbein sweaters.

Village Kidz

3 Charles Street 807-8542
Hours: Monday through Friday 12 P.M. to 7:30 P.M.; Saturday and Sunday 12 P.M. to 7 P.M
Return Policy: Store credit only.

Village Kidz sells attractive everyday wear and dressy clothes for boys and girls, newborn to age 12. It's pricey for everyday play clothes, with T-shirts at about $20 and dresses $50 and up. The clothes are stylish and include Chloe's Closet, Jean Bourget, and Cow & Lizard. Shoe brands include Shoe Be Doo, Right Step, Baby Botte, and Rebels. Village Kidz also sells stuffed bears from the Muffy Bear Collection.

Z'Baby Company*

100 West 72nd Street 579-BABY
Hours: Monday through Saturday 10:30 A.M. to 8:30 P.M.; Sunday 12 P.M.to 7 P.M.
Return Policy: Store credit only. No returns on

sale items.

At this Upper West Side store, you'll find a particularly good layette department—and the owner, a new mom herself, will work with you to put together the layette of your dreams. Bumper sets here are striking; and the clothing for newborns and toddlers is predominately trendy and on the expensive side. For little girls, you will find adorable velour and lace dresses by Baby Lulu; the highlight for boys is a Harley Davidson leather motorcycle jacket. Other brands sold here include Zutano, Trumpette, Baby Steps, Petit Bateau, Replay & Sons, and Baby Gigi.

Zitomer

969 Madison Avenue at 75th Street

737-2037

Hours: Monday through Friday 9 A.M. to 8 P.M.; Saturday 9 A.M. to 7 P.M.; Sunday 10 A.M. to 6 P.M..

Return Policy: Refund with receipt within ten days.

With convenient shopping hours and a flexible return policy, every neighborhood would be lucky to have a store like this one. Clothing sizes range from newborn to fourteen years, and brands available include Petit Bateau, Florian, Aletta, Carter's, Sophie Dess, Mini Basix, Mini Man, Joseph Baby, and Galipette. The service is good, and the prices and selection are excellent.

RESALE SHOPS

Here's where you'll find real bargains—the big names, hardly worn, at prices way below those of the boutiques.

Good-Byes Children's Resale Shop

230 East 78th Street 794-2301

Open every day; call for hours.

Return Policy: Store credit only.

This is the newest of the resale shops, and one of the nicest. Clothing here ranges from $5 to $40, with the average price of a baby outfit around $10. The store has a play area for kids with coloring books and crayons.

First & Second Cousin New and Resale Children's Shop

142 Seventh Avenue at 10th Street

929-8048

Hours: Monday through Saturday 11 A.M. to 7 P.M.; Sunday 12 P.M. to 6 P.M.

Return Policy: Store credit only.

This shop offers mostly new (some funky) clothing with brands like Flapdoodles and Mulberry Bush for newborns to size 14. The selection of resale clothing is small, but clean. Prices are about half those of their new merchandise.

Once Upon A Time
171 East 92nd Street 831-7619
Hours: Monday through Saturday 10 A.M. to 6 P.M.; Closed Sunday.
Return Policy: Store credit only.

This resale shop carries beautiful clothing for resale as well as some new clothes at deep discounts. You can find new dresses here for $150 that cost $375 at a Madison Avenue boutique! Lots of gently worn Gap clothes and toddler size jeans for $8. Sizes range from newborn to size 12.

Second Act
1046 Madison Avenue at 79th Street
2nd Floor 988-2440
Hours: Tuesday through Saturday 9 A.M. to 5 P.M.; Closed Sunday and Monday.
Return Policy: Store credit only.

Savvy shoppers can find clothing here from Sears to Bon Point. The store carries many European designer dresses and party clothes for girls and boys. Sizes range from newborn to pre-teen.

The Thrift Shop
62 Thomas Street at Church Street 571-2644
Hours: Tuesday through Thursday 11 A.M. to 2 P.M.; Friday 11 A.M. to 4 P.M.; Closed Saturday, Sunday, and Monday.
Return Policy: No returns.

This shop offers great bargains on children's clothes, with most items priced from $1 to $6. There can be lots from Baby Gap, as well as some pretty outfits from Laura Ashley.

MALLS

Consider the possibility of leaving town from time to time to do your children's clothes shopping—find bargains, skip the sales tax, or enjoy strolling your baby around an air-conditioned mall on a hot and sticky New York day. We list malls in the tri-state area that have several children's stores and are within an hour or so of the city. All driving directions are from New York City.

Many of the mall stores have been

described throughout this chapter. Brief descriptions of the stores not previously mentioned are provided here.

Northern New Jersey

Fashion Center

Route 17 and Ridgewood Avenue

Paramus, NJ 201-444-9050

Hours: Monday through Saturday 10 A.M. to 9:30 P.M.; Closed Sunday.

Directions: Take the George Washington Bridge to Route 4 West. Take Route 4 to Route 17N and Ridgewood Avenue.

Stores:

Denny's*: A terrific selection of fashionable play clothes for newborns to teens. All clothing is discounted from ten to fifty percent. Pamela makes seasonal trips here to stock up on pajamas, socks, tights, and accessories for Rebecca and Benjamin.

Noodle Kidoodle*: A terrific toy store stocked with an outstanding selection of educational toys, games, tapes, art supplies, and more.

Discovery Zone: An indoor play space.

Jenny John Shoes: A children's store with shoes from the first walker to teens.

Paramus Park Mall

Route 17, Paramus, NJ 201-261-8000

Hours: Monday through Saturday 10 A.M. to 9:30 P.M.; Closed Sunday.

Directions: Take the George Washington Bridge to Route 80 West, stay on Route 80 until you reach the Garden State Parkway North (Exit 163). Take the Garden State to Route 17N. Go 1/2 mile, and you will see two entrances to the mall in the northbound lane.

Stores:

The Children's Place

Gap Kids

Gymboree

Garden State Plaza Mall

Route 17 South, Paramus, NJ 201-843-2404

Hours: Monday through Saturday 10 A.M. to 9:30 P.M.; Closed Sunday.

Directions: Take the George Washington Bridge to Route 4 West. Take Route 4 to Route 17 South, go 100 yards past the Route 4 interchange, and make a right into the mall entrance.

Stores:

Dine-A-Shirt: for casual and sporty T-shirts and sweatshirts.

Gymboree
Lapin House: a European boutique.
Gap Kids.

Riverside Square Mall
Route 4 West, Hackensack, NJ
201-489-2212
Hours: Monday through Saturday 10 A.M. to 9:30 P.M.; Closed Sunday.

Directions: Take the George Washington Bridge to Route 4. The mall is on the right-hand side of the street, past the Hackensack exit.

Stores:

A Pea in the Pod
Gap Kids
La Petite Gaminerie: Reasonably priced European clothing from play clothes to holiday items.
Lapin House
Laura Ashley Mother & Child:* Long dresses with flowery designs for baby girls and their moms.
Ralph Lauren/Polo: Preppy clothing—polo shirts, khaki pants, and high-quality jeans, T-shirts, and sweaters. Clothing is on the moderate end of designer prices.

United Colors of Benetton: A European-style clothing store for infants and older. The clothes are brightly colored, and almost all are 100 percent cotton.

Westchester

The Westchester
Bloomingdale Road, White Plains, NY
914-683-8600
Hours: Monday through Saturday 10 A.M. to 9 P.M.; Sunday 11 A.M. to 6 P.M.

Directions: Take the Hutchinson River Parkway or I 95 North to 287 West. Take 287 to Westchester Avenue (Exit 8). Make a left onto Bloomingdale Road for parking at The Westchester.

Stores:

Baby Guess
Gap Kids
Lapin House
Gymboree
Jacadi
Talbots Kids & Babies.

Woodbury Commons Mall

Harriman, NY 914-928-4000

Hours: Monday through Saturday 10 A.M. to 8 P.M.

Directions: Take the upper level of the George Washington Bridge; make a right onto the Palisades Parkway North. Take the Palisades to Harriman (Exit 16). Immediately after the toll, you will see the mall entrance.

Stores: *All stores here are discount stores and/or outlets.

Carter's: This store features simple cotton clothing, including baby sleepwear. It is the perfect place to purchase layette clothes at a discount.

Genuine Kids: The clothing starts at twelve months and goes up to size 16, with an emphasis on outerwear.

Maternity Works: Clothes are thirty to seventy-five percent off original prices.

Mighty Mac Children's Clothing and Shoes: Clothing, shoes, and sneakers for newborns through two-year-olds. You'll find Looney Toons sports jackets, Barney items, socks, tights, and more.

Oshkosh B'Gosh

Polly Flinders: Traditional children's wear for newborns to size 16. Their casual line, Today's Child, is less expensive and makes good play clothes. They also carry accessories such as hair ribbons, suspenders, and socks.

Toy Liquidators: A closeout store offering name brand toys discounted fifty to seventy-five percent.

Long Island

Roosevelt Field Shopping Center

Glen Cove, NY, 516-742-8000

Hours: Monday through Saturday 10 A.M. to 9 P.M.; Sunday 11 A.M. to 6 P.M.

Directions: Take the Long Island Expressway to the Northern State Parkway (Exit 38). Take the Northern State to the Meadowbrook Parkway, and get off at Exit M2, Mall Exit. The mall will be directly in front of you.

Stores:

The Children's Place

Disney Store

FAO Schwarz

Gap Kids

Gymboree

Kay-Bee Toys

Noodle Kidoodle

United Colors of Benetton

Sunrise Mall

Sunrise Highway, Massapequa, NY
516-795-3225
*Hours: Monday through Saturday 10 A.M. to
9:30 P.M.; Sunday 11 A.M. to 6 P.M.*

Directions: Take the Long Island
Expressway to Route 110 South. Get off at
Sunrise Highway (Exit 27 West). Go down two
street lights and make a right. The mall is on
Sunrise Highway.

Stores:

The Children's Place,

Disney Store

Gap Kids

Kay-Bee Toys

Lobel's Stride Rite

Noodle Kidoodle

Walt Whitman Mall

Dix Hills, NY 516-271-1741
*Hours: Monday through Saturday 10 A.M. to
9:30 P.M.; Sunday 11 A.M. to 6 P.M.*

Directions: Take the Long Island
Expressway to Route 110 (Exit 49 North).
Take Route 110 north five miles; the mall is
on the right-hand side of Route 110.

Stores:

The Children's Place

Disney Store

Gap Kids

Gymboree

Mimi Maternity

Connecticut

Stamford Town Center

Tresser Boulevard, Stamford, CT
203-324-0935
*Hours: Monday through Friday 10 A.M.
to 9 P.M.; Saturday 10 A.M. to 6 P.M.;
Sunday 11 P.M. to 6 P.M.*

Directions: Take I 95 North to Exit 8.
Make a left at the first light, Atlantic Street.
Go to the third traffic light and make a right
onto Tresser Boulevard. From Tresser
Boulevard, make a left into the mall entrance.

Stores:

A Pea in the Pod

Baby Guess

Disney Store

FAO Schwarz

Gap Kids

Gymboree

Jacadi

Kay-Bee Toys

Kids Foot Locker

Lapin House

Laura Ashley Mother and Child

Mimi Maternity

Motherhood Maternity

Shoe Box*

11 · toys, toys, toys

You're about to rediscover the magic of toys, because you're going to be playing with them more than you can imagine. Having a baby is a great excuse to act like a kid again, and New York's toy stores, from the legendary F.A.O. Schwarz to the tiniest neighborhood specialist, can help you remember what it was like when a toy store was the greatest place in the world.

Of course, the world (even of toys) has changed since you were a kid, so here are some tips to get you started on picking the right toys, including where to find them. Have fun!

Toys must be safe, durable, and age appropriate—no buttons, long strings, ribbons, or small parts for children under three years of age. If a toy or toy part can fit through the cardboard center of a toilet paper roll, it's too small.

❄ If you're looking for a specific item, call ahead. Some stores will gift wrap and deliver nearby, so you might be able to shop over the phone.

❄ Pay attention to return policies and store credits. Some stores, like FAO Schwarz and Toys "R" Us, have an "anything, anytime" return policy, which can be useful if your youngster, like Alexander on his first birthday, receives three Barney dolls.

AGE-SPECIFIC TOYS
Newborn to 6 months

At this age, your child will begin to distinguish colors and shapes. He will enjoy objects that rattle or make a soothing noise.

Mobile and Musical Crib Light
   (Crib Essentials)
Wiggle Worm (Early Development)
Gymini/Gymfinity (Today's Kids)
Activity Arch (Fisher-Price)
Activity Links Playset (Fisher-Price)
Playmate (Fisher-Price or Sesame Street)

6 to 12 months

By this age, your baby will be moving around more: sitting up, rolling over, creeping, crawling, and almost walking. He will like toys that move, bounce, pop, and rattle. He will start to understand "cause and effect," will want to make things happen, and will enjoy doing the same things over and over again.

Activity Table (Fisher-Price)
Red Rings (Early Development)
Sesame Street Popping Pals (Playskool)
See and Say (Mattel)
Activity Walker (Fisher-Price)
Stacking Rings (Fisher-Price)
Exersaucer (Evenflo)

12 to 18 months

Your tot is learning to stack and build. He will also enjoy anything that moves along with him—cars and trucks to zoom along the floor, ducks and dogs to pull, and ride-on toys.

Popcorn Popper (Fisher-Price)
Push About Popper (Little Tikes)
Stacking-Nesting Blocks (Mother Goose)
Baby's First Blocks (Fisher-Price)
Sport Coupe (Little Tikes)
Bubble Mower (Fisher-Price)
Melody Push Chime (Fisher-Price)
Dolls or stuffed animals
Baby doll stroller

18 to 24 months

Your toddler is on the go, curious, and creative. Coloring books, paint sets, simple puzzles, and moving toys will fascinate her.

Little People School (Fisher-Price)
Toddler Tots School Bus (Little Tikes)
Trucks, cars, and dolls
Loop d' Loop Wooden Beads
Toddler Tots Dump Truck (Little Tikes)
Puzzles (Guidecraft, Simplex, or
   Ravensburger)

THE STORES

A Bear's Place*

789 Lexington Avenue at 61st Street

826-6465

Hours: Monday through Friday 9 A.M. to 7 P.M.; Saturday 9 A.M. to 6 P.M.; Sunday 10 A.M. to 5 P.M.; closed Sunday in August.

Return Policy: Store credit only.

This friendly shop has a good selection of educational toys for children under five years old. There are spelling board games, a Velcro rainbow board, musical instruments, puzzles, and a wonderful puppet theater. A Bear's Place has a large selection of upholstered furniture and personalized items, too. All toys sold here are JPMA approved. Gift wrap.

Mary Arnold Toys

962 Lexington Avenue at 70th Street

744- 8510

Hours: Monday through Friday 9 A.M. to 6 P.M.; Saturday 10 A.M. to 5 P.M.; Sunday 10 A.M. to 6 P.M.; closed Sunday in the summer.

Return Policy: Refunds with a receipt within thirty days; otherwise store credit only.

A neighborhood favorite for decades, here you'll find the fine brands from Fisher-Price to Madame Alexander, as well as videos, games, dolls, puppets, and arts and crafts galore. The personable staff can create party favor bags or a special gift basket. Free gift wrap and local delivery.

Children of Paradise

154 Bleeker Street at Thompson Street

473-7148

Hours: Monday through Saturday 11 A.M. to 7 P.M.; Sunday 12 P.M. to 7 P.M.

Return Policy: Store credit only.

Toys for babies and young children include dolls, simple art supplies, and books. There's a larger selection for older children, including model kits and comic books.

The Children's General Store

2473 Broadway at 92nd Street 580-2723

Hours: Monday through Saturday 10 A.M. to 6 P.M.; Sunday 12 P.M. to 5 P.M.

Return Policy: Store credit only.

This very small shop, downstairs at West Side Playspace, carries an appealing selection, from puppets to cards, books, and tutus. For older children there are musical instruments, how-to kits, doll house furniture by Ambi, and Plan toys. Free gift wrap.

Classic Toys

218 Sullivan Street at Third Avenue
674-4434
Hours: Tuesday through Sunday 12 P.M.
to 6:30 P.M.; closed Monday.
Return Policy: Store credit only.

A unique mix of vintage and new toys, including toy soldiers, miniature cars, figurines, and well-known characters (Star Trek, Disney), as well as a selection of dinosaurs, farm animals, and stuffed animals.

Cute Toonz

372 Fifth Avenue at 35th Street 967-6942
Hours: Monday through Saturday 8 A.M.
to 9 P.M.; Sunday 9 A.M. to 8 P.M.
Return Policy: Store credit only within three weeks.

Lots of great Disney, Sesame Street, and other cartoon characters in all shapes and forms. Shop here for T-shirts, knapsacks, cups, stuffed animals, watches, and Hello Kitty accessories. A great place for small gifts and party favors.

Dinosaur Hill

302 East 9th Street 473-5850
Hours: Monday through Sunday 11 A.M.
to 7 P.M.
Return Policy: Liberal.

This specialty toy and clothing store has quality marbles, marionettes, mobiles, T. C. Timber toys, and handcrafted toys from around the world. It also carries clothing, including an extraordinary selection of hats, mostly for children ages two to six. Free gift wrap.

The Disney Store

711 Fifth Avenue at 55th Street 702-0702
39 West 34th Street 279-9890
147 Columbus Avenue at 66th Street
362-2386
210 West 42nd Street at Seventh Avenue
221-0430
Hours: Monday through Saturday 10 A.M.
to 8 P.M.; Sunday 11 A.M. to 6 P.M.
Return Policy: Refund with receipt.

You and your youngster will have a lot of fun browsing through the colorful displays of every Disney character you've ever heard of—and probably a few you haven't— in the form of stuffed animals, videos, books, figurines, art kits, and clothing. Gift boxes are free; gift wrapping is $5 per gift.

The Enchanted Forest*

85 Mercer Street 925-6677

Hours: Monday through Saturday 11 A.M. to 7 P.M.; Sunday 12 P.M. to 6 P.M.

Return Policy: Store credit only.

Walk in, and you and your little one are in a forest complete with trees, bridges, and waterfalls. The woodland decor and classical music create a peaceful ambiance for browsing. Explore the selection of handmade toys from all over the world: magnetic play theaters from Czechoslovakia, animal whistles from India, puzzles from Egypt and Greece, wooden toys and rattles. You'll also find blocks, books, and plush stuffed animals. Free gift wrap.

FAO Schwarz*

767 Fifth Avenue at 58th Street 644-9400

Hours: Monday through Saturday 10 A.M. to 6 P.M.; Sunday 11 A.M. to 5 P.M.

Return Policy: Lenient.

FAO Schwarz, a city landmark and major tourist attraction, has the best and largest range of toys in the world, from gorgeous dolls (see the Barbie Boutique) to games, a jungle of stuffed animals, arts and crafts, classic toys, modern favorites, many exclusives, and all the hottest new rages (generally in stock). Huge, exciting, and kid-friendly, your child will love it. And so will Grandma. Yes, it's expensive, but seventy per cent of the toys here cost $50 or less. Free gift wrap.

Gepetto's Toy Box

161 Seventh Avenue South at Perry Street 620-7511

Hours: Monday through Thursday 11 A.M. to 8 P.M.; Friday and Saturday 11 A.M. to 10 P.M.; Sunday 1 P.M. to 7 P.M.

Return Policy: Store credit only.

A wonderful neighborhood store, Gepetto's carries toys by manufacturers like Ambi, Playmobile, Ziggy Kids, and others. It features a nice selection of musical mirrors, photo albums, and other specialty gifts. Free gift wrap.

Just Jakes*

40 Hudson Street at Duane Street 267-1716

Hours: Monday through Friday 11 A.M.

to 5 P.M.; Saturday 11 A.M. to 6 P.M.; Sunday
12 P.M. to 5 P.M.
Return Policy: Store credit only.

Children can play with many of the toys,
take an arts and crafts class, or listen to a
story hour. All the products are educational
and creative—no war toys or battery-operated
items. This wonderful store will deliver anywhere the subway goes. Free gift wrap.

Kay-Bee Toys

901 Avenue of the Americas at 34th Street
629-5386
Hours: Monday through Saturday 10 A.M.
to 8 P.M.; Sunday 10 A.M. to 6 P.M.
Return Policy: Refund with receipt within thirty
days, otherwise store credit only.

Kay-Bee Toys is a chain with shops in
many malls. It carries the most popular name
brands, as well as arts-and-crafts and water
toys. This is the place to find the hot toy of
the moment. Prices are usually discounted.

Kidding Around*

68 Bleeker Street at Broadway 598-0228
60 West 15th Street 645-6337
Hours: Monday through Saturday 10 A.M.

(15th Street) or 11 A.M. (Bleeker Street)
to 7 P.M.; Sunday 11 A.M. to 6 P.M.
Return Policy: Store credit only.

Kidding Around, a downtown fave, has
a small infant section with black and white rattles, mobiles and squishy toys, and a larger
selection of toys for one- to eight-year-olds.
There are unique puppet theaters, musical
instruments, Native American and African
American dolls, and a very nice Italian doll
line. You'll find Brio, Ambi, Battat, and Playmobile here, as well as beach balls, some classic tapes, videos, and books. Free gift wrap.

Little Extras*

550 Amsterdam Avenue at 86th Street
721-6161
Hours: Monday through Friday 10 A.M.
to 6:30 P.M.; Saturday 10 A.M. to 6 P.M.;
Closed Sunday.
Return Policy: Store credit only.

Pretty, roomy, and inviting, Little Extras
is a great source for gifts. There are black-
and-white toys for newborns, bibs with cute
sayings, and the educational New Beginnings
line. In addition, the store carries some furniture, including stools, chairs, and toy chests;

the best quality bathrobes and towels for children; and junior-size suitcases and umbrellas. Free gift wrap and personalizing.

Little Rickie

49 First Avenue at Third Street 505-6467

Hours: Monday through Saturday 11 A.M. to 8 P.M.; Sunday 12 P.M. to 7 P.M.

Return Policy: Store credit only.

Although this store sells stuffed animals, mobiles, and children's books, it's not a conventional toy store. Everything at Little Rickie is unique, classic, handmade, vintage, and original. Little Rickie is a real one-of-a-kind New York shop with lots of 1950s memorabilia. Stop in to hunt for grown-up toys and gifts as well. Free gift wrap.

My Favorite Place

265 West 87th Street 362-5320

Hours: Monday through Saturday 9:30 A.M. to 6:30 P.M.; Sunday 10:00 A.M. to 6:30 P.M.

Return Policy: Store credit only.

My Favorite Place is an indoor play space as well as a toy store. The store has a big selection of arts and crafts projects and puzzles, plus brands of toys such as Battat, Ambi, and Playskool. Free gift wrap.

Ovations

Two World Financial Center, 225 Liberty Street

791-9300

Hours: Monday through Friday 10:30 A.M. to 6 P.M.; Saturday 12 P.M. to 5 P.M.; closed Sunday.

Return Policy: Store credit only.

Ovations prepares custom-made gift baskets of all kinds; their newborn baskets are particularly impressive, whether you spend $50 or $500. The staff is helpful and the quality of the clothing and merchandise is superb. Phone orders accepted. Free gift wrap.

Penny Whistle Toys*

1283 Madison Avenue at 91st Street

369-3868

448 Columbus Avenue at 81st Street

873-9090

Hours: Monday, Tuesday, Wednesday, Friday 9 A.M. to 6 P.M.; Thursday 9 A.M. to 7 P.M.; Saturday 10 A.M. to 6 P.M.; Sunday 11 A.M. to 5 P.M.

Return Policy: Store credit only.

220 · city baby

These are terrific toy stores known for their commitment to high quality and their unique toys and games. Penny Whistle carries many top-of-the line brands like Ambi, Brio, Playmobile, Koosh, Corolle, Madame Alexander, and Disney. Great games, puzzles, and arts-and-crafts kits are available, too. The friendly, easygoing staff will help you find the perfect age-appropriate gift, and wrapping is free. There is also a location on Route 27 in Bridgehampton.

Promises Fulfilled

1592 Second Avenue at 81st Street

472-1600

Hours: Monday through Saturday 10 A.M. to 6 P.M.; Closed Sunday.

437 Third Avenue at 30th Street 679-0006

Hours: Monday through Saturday 10 A.M. to 7 P.M.; Closed Sunday.

Return Policy: Store credit only.

You'll find a varied selection for babies and lots of choices when you need a birthday present for an older child (from costumes to construction kits). You can also buy personalized and coordinated accessories for your child's room: benches, frames, clocks, coat racks, mirrors, lamps, and even diaper pails. Cute baby

books and photo albums are a specialty here. There is another store on Newtown Lane in East Hampton. Free gift wrap.

Quest Toys

Two World Financial Center, 225 Liberty Street

945-9330

Hours: Monday through Saturday 10 A.M. to 7 P.M.; Sunday 11 A.M. to 6 P.M.

Return Policy: Store credit only.

This small store is welcome shopping for working parents in the Wall Street area. Popular brands sold here include Holgate, T. C. Timber, Thomas the Tank, and Radio Flyer. There are also wooden train sets, children's books, videos and cassettes, puppets, plush toys, letter blocks, clay, chalk, and more. Free gift wrap.

Noodle Kidoodle

112 East 86th Street 427-6611

Hours: Monday through Friday 10 A.M. to 7 P.M.; Saturday 10 A.M. to 6 P.M.; Sunday 11 A.M. to 5 P.M.

Return Policy: Refund with a receipt, otherwise store credit only.

What a great selection! This big toy store has fair prices on all the most popular brands, and carries puzzles, games, a large selection of educational toys, arts-and-crafts supplies, and more. It also has two computers for toddlers to play with, and a toy train set up in the middle of the store.

Toys "R" Us

1293 Broadway at 34th Street 594-8697

Hours: Monday, Thursday, and Friday, 9 A.M. to 9 P.M.; Tuesday and Saturday 9 A.M. to 8 P.M.; Sunday 11 A.M. to 7 P.M.

24-30 Union Square East 674-8697

Hours: Monday through Saturday 9 A.M. to 8 P.M.; Sunday 10 A.M. to 7 P.M.

Return Policy: Refund with a receipt, otherwise store credit only.

Toys "R" Us discounts every well-known name-brand toy. It carries a lot of Fisher-Price, Safety 1st, Playskool, and Mattel; these are all the latest toys, and the prices and selection are usually the best in town.

Uncle Futz

408 Amsterdam Avenue at 79th Street

799-6723

Hours: Monday through Friday 10:30 AM. to 6:30 P.M.; Saturday 10 A.M. to 5 P.M.; Sunday 10 A.M. to 5:45 P.M.

Return Policy: Store credit only. Personalized items or jewelry are final sale.

Uncle Futz is a great place to browse and shop for clever picture frames, piggy banks, bathrobes, towels, step stools, easels, bulletin boards, and jewelry. They sell toys from Chicco and Ambi as well as creative kits and books. Moreover, they make party favor bags and will personalize gifts. Free gift wrap.

Vermont Teddy Bear

538 Madison Avenue at 54th Street

688-9394

Hours: Monday through Friday 10 A.M. to 7 P.M.; Saturday 10 A.M. to 6 P.M.; Sunday 12 P.M. to 5 P.M.

Return Policy: Refund with receipt; otherwise store credit.

This is *the* place if you're shopping for a very special teddy bear. Vermont Teddy Bear stocks plush bears in all shapes, sizes, and colors. Their gift baskets are especially cute.

Warner Bros. Store

1 East 57th Street 754-0300

Hours: Monday through Saturday 10 A.M. to 8 P.M.; Sunday 11 A.M. to 6 P.M.

Return Policy: Refund with receipt, otherwise store credit only.

With a café, a 3-D movie theater, and interactive games, this nine-story store offers entertainment as well as shopping. As you might expect, it's a world of Bugs Bunny, Tweety Bird, Scoobie-doo, and other Warner Brothers–related toys, stuffed animals, clothing, and accessories. The mail-order service offers free gift wrap.

West Side Kids*

498 Amsterdam Avenue at 84th Street
496-7282
Hours: Monday through Saturday 10 A.M. to 7 P.M.; Sunday 12 P.M. to 6 P.M.
Return Policy: Store credit only.

This is a terrific neighborhood store, with excellent service and a varied selection of educational toys, quality books, and "imagination" items for playing pretend, such as miniature brooms, rakes, and kitchen utensils. There is also a selection of puzzles plus a great assortment of small toys for party favors. Check out the schedule of free, in-store kiddy events, such as face-painting. Free gift wrap.

Zitomer

969 Madison Avenue at 76th Street
737-2037
Hours: Monday through Friday 9 A.M. to 7:45 P.M.; Saturday 9 A.M. to 6:45 P.M.; Sunday 10 A.M. to 5:45 P.M.
Return Policy: Refund with receipt within ten days, otherwise store credit only.

It looks like a pharmacy downstairs, yet upstairs it is a treasure trove of children's toys and beautiful clothing. You'll find dolls, puzzles, books, arts and crafts, videos, games, and toys including Battat, Ambi, Brio, Fisher-Price, and V-Tech. The store will ship and deliver locally. Free gift wrap.

12 · books, videos, audios, catalogs, and magazines

City babies love city bookstores. That's where they can listen to stories while their moms pick out videos, audios, magazines, and, of course, books. The whole world of baby culture—written, spoken, and visual—is really exciting today. Wonderful artists and musicians are creating lasting treasures for your children, and it's going to be a great adventure for your family to discover all of them.

In this section you'll find a guide to New York's children's bookstores and all they hold, from the classic must-haves for children, like *Goodnight Moon*, to *Practical Parenting Tips* for you. We recommend favorite audio tapes that are sure to make a long car ride smoother, and videos that entertain and provide a few minutes of peace, or offer you helpful information about parenting. For those who love to get their tips from magazines, you'll learn about some of the best. And now that you're destined to spend more time at home, you can easily get your shopping done through any one of these catalogs offering terrific children's toys, clothing, and accessories.

BEST BOOKSTORES FOR CHILDREN

Bank Street Bookstore*

610 West 112th Street

678-1654

Hours: Monday through Thursday 10 A.M. to 8 P.M.; Friday and Saturday 10 A.M. to 6 P.M.; Sunday 12 P.M. to 5 P.M.

Return Policy: Store credit only.

With more than 40,000 titles for children, parents, and educators, Bank Street Bookstore is perhaps the best resource in the city for children's books. The knowledgeable staff can guide you on age-appropriate books.

Barnes & Noble

Locations throughout the city.

Hours: 9 A.M. to 11 P.M. most days; call for hours at the store nearest you.

Return Policy: Generous.

Barnes & Noble has an enormous selection. Its children's sections are comfortable, with plenty of room to sit and read with your child. Call to find out about story times and author appearances, particularly at Barnes & Noble Junior stores.

Books of Wonder

16 West 18th Street

989-3270

Hours: Monday through Saturday 11 A.M. to 7 P.M.; Sunday 11:30 A.M. to 6 P.M.

Return Policy: Store credit only.

This very special children's bookstore carries new, out-of-print, vintage, and rare books, with a section devoted to the Wizard of Oz and a great selection of illustrated books. No television or movie tie-ins, however, meaning no Barney- or Sesame Street-type books. Call for information on story hours.

Tootsie's Children's Books

554 Hudson Street at Perry Street

242-0182

Hours: Monday through Sunday 11 A.M. to 6 P.M.

Return Policy: Store credit only.

This recently-opened store offers new and classic toys, early development toys, puzzles, puppets, and educational games—all in addition to books for children and titles on parenting.

BEST BOOKS FOR BABIES AND TODDLERS

Books for babies are great fun, and there are hundreds of titles available. Many come in a variety of sizes, shapes, and formats—you can buy the perennial favorite *Goodnight Moon*, for example, in hardcover, paperback, and as a board book (with thick cardboard pages) that is easy for toddlers to hold.

You'll find bath books that can go into the tub with your youngster, and cloth books that are nice for your baby to play with in the crib. You'll find touch-and-feel books like *Pat the Bunny*; books that squeak (Disney has a great line); books about colors, numbers, and animals.

Of course, the greatest pleasure for your little one will be sitting on Mom or Dad's lap, pointing to the pictures, helping turn the pages, and listening to the story. Even while your child is still an infant, it's worthwhile to spend time each day reading aloud to him.

Here's a rundown of our favorite books, all suitable for reading to or with your baby or toddler:

Classics

Goodnight Moon* by Margaret Wise Brown

A timeless picture book with a charming story told in simple rhyming phrases.

The Little Engine that Could* by Watty Piper

How fast can you say, "I think I can, I think I can?"

Pat the Bunny* by Dorothy Kunhardt

Your child will love touching the soft bunny and Daddy's scratchy face.

The Very Hungry Caterpillar* by Eric Carle

A beautiful, interactive picture book about a caterpillar who eats and eats and turns into a butterfly.

Very First Mother Goose by Rosemary Wells

A rhyming book for the very young.

Popular Series and Authors

Dr. Seuss beginner books

*(One Fish, Two Fish, Red Fish, Blue Fish, etc.)**

Silly, rhyming stories with amusing drawings and creative characters.

Helen Oxenbury books

(All Fall Down; Clap Hands; Say Goodnight; Tickle, Tickle)

Babies love the simple rhyming phrases and pictures of other babies.

Madeline books by Ludwig Bemelmans

(Madeline; Madeline in London; Madeline's Rescue; etc.)*

If you have a City Baby, you might as well introduce her to Paris early.

My First Look at . . . books

(Colors; Numbers; Shapes; etc.)

There are more than fifteen books in this series, all of which include bright photographs of objects that kids will recognize.

Neil Ricklen books

(Mommy & Me; Daddy & Me; Baby's Big & Little)*

One word per page with engaging photographs of babies.

Paddington books by Michael Bond and John Lobban

(Paddington; Paddington's Colors; Paddington's ABC's; etc.)

Colorfully illustrated adventures of Paddington Bear, with only one word per page.

Richard Scarry books

(Lowly Worm Word Book, etc.)*

Scarry uses words and illustrations to create detailed worlds that fascinate children of any age.

Sandra Boynton books

(One, Two, Three; A to Z; Moo, Baa, La La La; The Going to Bed Book; Hippos Go Berserk; etc.)*

Rhyming sentences with cute cartoon pictures of animals.

Spot books by Eric Hill

(Spot Looks at Colors; Spot Looks at Shapes, etc.)*

Even babies can lift-the-flap to look for this adorable puppy and his friends.

BEST BOOKS FOR PARENTS

As a new mother, you'll want to stock your shelves with books by experts such as Penelope Leach, Dr. Spock, and T. Barry Brazelton. Here are a few more titles.

GENERAL

The Amazing Newborn by M. Klaus and J. Kennell

The Parent's Guide to Baby and Child Medical Care by Terril H. Hart, M.D.

The Pediatrician's Best Baby Planner for the First Year of Life by Daniel W. Dubner, M.D. and D. Gregory Felch, M.D.

Practical Parenting for the 21st Century by Julie Ross*

Your Baby's First Three Years by Dr. Paula Kelly

Games Babies Play by Julie Hagstrom and Joan Morrill*

Mother's Almanac by Marguerite Kelly and Elia S. Parsons*

Practical Parenting Tips by Vicki Lansky

Solve Your Children's Sleep Problems by Richard Ferber*

25 Things Every New Mother Should Know by Martha Sears, R.N. and William Sears, M.D.*

BREASTFEEDING

The Complete Book of Breastfeeding by Marvin S. Eiger, M.D. and Sally Wendklos Olds

Successful Breastfeeding by Nancy Dana and Anne Price

The Womanly Art of Breastfeeding by La Leche League*

TODDLERS

Kids Book to Welcome a New Baby by Barbara J. Collman

The Smart Parents' Guide to Kids T.V. by Milton Chen, Ph.D.

How to Take Great Trips with Your Kids by Sanford and Joan Portnoy

SPECIAL INTEREST

Twins from Conception to Five Years by Averil Clegg and Anne Woolett

The Single Mother's Book: A Practical Guide to Managing Your Children, Career, Home, Finances, and Everything Else by Joan Anderson

In Praise of Single Parents by Shoshana Alexander

Adoption Is for Always by Linda Walvoord Girard

We Adopted You Benjamin Koo by Linda Walvoord Girard

Almost all the super stores and many toy stores often have children's entertainment videos as well as grown-up videos covering a range of topics concerning new parents, such as breastfeeding, child development, and baby proofing. HMV, Tower Records, Coconuts, Blockbuster Video, and Champagne Video also sell and rent children's and parenting videos. Champagne Video is especially reasonable—two movies for $1.50, with a well-stocked children's section. There are four locations in Manhattan—three on the Upper East Side and one on the West Side. For a location near you, call 517-8700.

BEST VIDEOS FOR CHILDREN

During your child's first two or three years, at different times he is going to be madly in love with Barney, Big Bird, Ernie, Winnie-the-Pooh, or some character that hasn't even been invented yet. You'll be renting or buying any number of videos featuring these lovable creatures, even if, like Kelly, you once swore no child of yours would ever spend an hour watching a purple dinosaur.

Here's a listing of videos based on popular television series (the titles give you an idea of what each is about); Disney feature films now on video; and a few more tapes offering fun or instruction:

BARNEY (BEST FOR NINE MONTHS AND UP)

Barney's Alphabet Zoo
*Barney's Birthday**
*Let's Pretend with Barney**
Riding in Barney's Car
*Barney and Mother Goose**
And more …

DISNEY'S SPOT SERIES (BEST FOR NEWBORNS TO NINE MONTHS)

Spot Goes to the Farm

*Spot Goes to School**

*Where's Spot?**

Sweet Dreams Spot

DISNEY CLASSICS (BEST FOR AGE TWO AND UP)

Aladdin

A Goofy Movie

Cinderella

The Fox and the Hound

The Great Mouse Detective

The Lion King

Pocahontas

Snow White and the Seven Dwarfs

One Hundred and One Dalmatians

The Aristocats

DISNEY'S WINNIE-THE-POOH SERIES (BEST FOR EIGHTEEN MONTHS AND UP)

Pooh Party

Pooh Learning

Cowboy Pooh

Sharing and Caring

*Making Friends**

*Winnie-the-Pooh and Tigger Too**

Winnie-the-Pooh and the Honey Tree

SESAME STREET (TWELVE MONTHS AND UP)

My Sesame Street Home Video Play-Along

Sesame Street Sing Along

Big Bird Sings

The Best of Bert and Ernie

Do the Alphabet

The Best of Elmo

Sing, Hoot & Howl with the Sesame Street Animals

Sesame Street's 25th Birthday Celebration

MISCELLANEOUS (EIGHTEEN MONTHS AND UP)

Baby Songs

Shari Lewis' "Don't Wake Your Mom!"

Wee Sing Grandpa's Magical Toys

*Richard Scarry's The Best Birthday Party Ever**

VIDEOS FOR PARENTS
Baby's Early Growth, Care, and Development

Baby's First Months 'What Do We Do Now?' Developed by twelve pediatricians, this video leads parents from birth through their baby's first few months. New parents are instructed on the daily care of a newborn.

The First Two Years—A Comprehensive Guide To Enhancing Your Child's Physical and Mental Development This award-winning video observes babies involved in everyday activities. The developmental periods are divided by age: one day to three months, three to six months, six to twelve months, and twelve to twenty-four months. Other topics include breastfeeding, early child care, infant nutrition, physical growth, and mobility/motor skills.

Dr. Jane Morton's Guide to Successful Breastfeeding Using a case study and graphics, this video shows the critical steps to comfortable, effective breastfeeding, including how to avoid common problems.

Touchpoints: The Definitive Video Series on Parenting, Volume 1: Pregnancy, Birth, and the First Weeks of Life* This practical guide to child development defines touchpoints as periods preceding rapid growth in learning, which are significant to future development. Points covered include pregnancy, delivery, preparation for birth, and the first weeks of your baby's life to three months.

Your Baby—A Video Guide To Care and Understanding with Penelope Leach A comprehensive and practical guide to newborn baby care and development, this video demonstrates techniques of everyday care in a variety of situations.

What Every Baby Knows—A Guide To Pregnancy An instructive video with sensible information concerning the development of children from birth to three months. This tape also explores a father's emotional involvement during pregnancy, gives a detailed profile of one couple's delivery, and looks at typical issues that arise in the early months after birth.

Exercise/Well-Being

Jane Fonda's Pregnancy, Birth, and Recovery This exercise program demonstrates pregnancy and recovery workouts, baby massage, and infant care, and skills to physically prepare for birth.

*Kathy Smith's Pregnancy Workout** Both mothers-to-be and three different childbirth experts instruct mothers on how to maintain their energy and strength. Divided into prenatal and postnatal sections, the ninety-minute tape covers exercise for the new mothers up to six weeks after giving birth.

Safety Videos

Barney Safety Barney and friends instruct little ones on safety with cars, traffic, and in the home.

Fire Safety for Kids with Beasel the Easel This video, endorsed by educators and firefighters, teaches basic fire safety to children age two and up. Children will enjoy the cast of characters and an original soundtrack.

*CPR To Save Your Child or Baby** This award-winning video carefully explains the step-by-step procedures of CPR, including instructions on the Heimlich maneuver and choking rescue. If you haven't had a chance to take a CPR-instruction class, this is the next best thing.

Infant and Toddler Emergency First Aid (Volume 1: Accidents, Volume 2: Illnesses) These videos are endorsed by the American Academy of Pediatrics. The tapes explain emergency medical services including the proper procedures and actions to take when giving CPR or dealing with choking or poisoning.

Mr. Baby Proofer A tape designed to teach parents how to make their home a baby-safe environment, this hands-on guide also describes key safety products.

Choosing Quality Child Care This video answers questions such as how to recognize quality child care, how to make sure a child is safe, and what to ask during an interview.

AUDIO CASSETTES FOR CHILDREN

Just because you have a baby doesn't mean you have to spend the next few years listening to terrible, sappy music. There's some really good music being written for children these days, and you'll be amazed to find yourself humming the tunes to yourself (even in the company of adults). In fact, you can find a lot of the adult music you like re-recorded for children. Much of the music recommended here is in *Baby's Best* by Susan Silver, or the *Music for Little People* catalog (800-727-2233).

RAFFI
Baby Beluga
*Bananaphone**
Singable Songs for the Very Young

JOANIE BARTEL
Joanie Bartel's award-winning sound really appeals. Tapes and CDs are available from Discovery Magic at 800-451-5175
*Lullaby Magic**
Bathtime Magic
*Dancin' Magic**
Morning Magic

SESAME STREET
Ernie's Side by Side
Sesame Street Silly Songs

OTHER SUGGESTIONS
A Child's Gift of Lullabies by Someday Baby
G'Night Wolfgang by Ric Louchard
*Hap Palmer's Follow Along Songs**
Hush-A-Bye Dreamsongs
Lullabies of Broadway by Mimi Bessette
Lullaby Berceuse by XYZ
Peter, Paul, and Mommy by Peter, Paul, and Mary*
Shakin' It by Parachute Express
Sleep, Baby Sleep by Nicolette Larson*

The Lullaby and Goodnight Sleep Kit
Sugar Beats
The Beatles for Kids

CHILDREN'S CATALOGS
Shopping by catalog can be the world's greatest convenience; there are loads of them, all filled with great things for babies and children. Here are a few of our favorites offering one-of-a-kind accessories, toys, and practical imported clothing not available in stores.

After the Stork
1501 12th Street NW
P.O. Box 26200
Albuquerque, NM 87104
800-333-5437
   Reasonably priced basics for toddlers and young boys and girls, including swimwear, rain gear, shoes, and everyday clothing.

Biobottoms
P.O. Box 6009
Petaluma, CA 94953
800-766-1254
707-778-7152 in California
   Cotton and dress-up clothing for infants, toddlers, and older children.

Childcraft
P.O. Box 29137
Overland Park
KS 66201
800-222-7725

Classic toys from blocks to easels to costumes.

Children's Wear
31333 Agoura Road
Westlake Village, CA 91361
800-242-5437

Children's Wear offers over 600 styles and colors of cotton basics, play clothes, and more.

Chinaberry Book Service*
2180 Range Way, Suite B
Spring Valley, CA 91978
800-776-2242

Chinaberry has wonderful books for children.

Constructive Playthings*
1227 East 119th Street
Grandview, MO 64030
800-832-0572

An array of colorful, entertaining toys

for young boys and girls, with a section called "First Playthings," that's especially good for newborns to one-year-olds.

Hand In Hand*
Catalog Center, Route 26
R.R. 1, Box 1425
Oxford, ME 04270-9711
800-872-9745

Toys, games, puzzles, and accessories for the young child or toddler, including items used for art, music, camping, traveling, and storage.

Hanna Anderson*
1010 NW Flanders Street
Portland, OR 97209
800-222-0544

Hanna Anderson carries moderately priced, superior quality cotton play clothes for young children, including swimwear and hats plus some matching outfits for parents.

The Natural Baby Catalog
816 Silvia Street, 800 B-S
Trenton, NJ 08628-3299
609-771-3299

The Natural Baby Catalog carries natural, ecological, and health-minded products, including cloth diaper covers, bedroom furniture, many beautifully crafted wooden toys, and books.

One Step Ahead*
P.O. Box 517
Lake Bluff, IL 60044
800-274-8440

One Step Ahead is good for baby products, including carriers/strollers, car seats, cribs, bottle holders, and some toys and clothing. Safety, travel, and mealtime helpers are also available.

Oshkosh B'Gosh
1112 Seventh Avenue, P.O. Box 2222
Monroe, WI 53566-8222
800-MY BGOSH (800-692-4674)

Oshkosh is simple all–American kid's wear, including classic denim overalls and jeans for your toddler or young child, in both boys' and girls' sizes.

Parenting and Family Life
P.O. Box 2153, Dept. PA7
Charleston, WV 25328
800-468-4227

Extensive selection of videos on parenting, discipline, and health-and-safety issues.

Patagonia Mail Order
P.O. Box 8900
Bozeman, MT 59715
800-336-9090

Patagonia is known for its own brand of rugged everyday clothing and parkas, as well as its cozy fleece jackets.

Perfectly Safe*
7245 Whipple Avenue, NW
North Canton, OH 44720
800-837-KIDS (800-837-5437)

Safety gates, bathtub spout covers, and other items to child-proof a home.

Playclothes
P.O. Box 29137
Overland Park
KS 66201-9137
800-362-7529

Traditional clothing with bear and puppy motifs; lots of basic T-shirts and sweatpants. Don't miss the collection of picture-perfect clothes for special occasions.

Play Fair Toys

P.O. Box 18210

Boulder, CO 80308

800-824-7255

Games, blocks, nesting animals, videos, and many other play items that just may help your little one learn to play fair.

Premiewear

6475 Ridge Place, Route 3

Twin Falls, ID 83301

800-992-8469

A selection of clothing that's sized for premature and low birthweight babies.

The Right Start Catalog*

Right Start Plaza

5334 Sterling Center Drive

Westlake, CA 91361-4627

800-LITTLE-1 (800-548-8531)

Nursery accessories, safe plastic toys, diaper bags, car seats, jogging strollers, baby carriers, and more.

Rubens & Marble Inc.

P.O. Box 14900

Chicago, IL 60614

773-348-6200

Rubens & Marble has basic white, 100 percent cotton clothing and bedding for infants. Excellent prices.

This Country's Toys*

Skaneateles, NY 13152

800-359-1233

This Country's Toys offers unique, American-made toys and games, with an emphasis on wood blocks and trains.

Toys to Grow On

P.O. Box 17, Long Beach, CA 90801

800-542-8338

All kinds of toys for newborn to pre-teens.

Troll's Learn & Play

100 Corporate Drive

Mahwah, NJ 07430

800-247-6106

Creative toys, costumes, activity books, videos, art supplies, and counting toys, mostly for ages two and up.

MAGAZINES FOR PARENTS

There's always something to do with kids in New York. Check these publications for monthly calendars plus services and helpful articles just for New York parents. Many are free at local shops. Here are some of the better ones.

Big Apple Parents' Paper

36 East 12th Street, New York, NY 10003
533-2277

This monthly publication features topical articles on parenting and kids. It has been around for over ten years and is an invaluable resource for Manhattan parents.

New York Family

141 Halstead Avenue, Suite 3D
Mamaroneck, NY 10543
914-381-7474

Started by two moms, this monthly magazine offers useful event calendars as well as features on everything from children's health to traveling with kids.

The Expectant & New Parents Guide

37 West 72nd Street
New York, NY 10023
595-4569

Think of this as a mini *What to Expect When You're Expecting*, geared especially toward New York parents.

Parent Guide

475 Park Avenue South
New York, NY 10022
213-8840

This monthly magazine is for New York families with young children offering information on schools, camps, entertainment, and more.

National Magazines

Two of our favorite magazines are *Parent's* and *Child*, but all those listed offer practical advice and information on parenting and child development.

American Baby

575 Lexington Avenue
New York, NY 10022
752-0775

A monthly magazine for expectant parents and parents of one-year-olds and under.

Baby Talk

185 Madison Avenue

New York, NY 10016
679-4400

A monthly magazine for expectant parents and parents of two-year-olds and under.

Child*
P.O. Box 3173, Harlan, IA 51593-2364
800-777-0222

A popular, authoritative magazine full of information for parents of newborns through teens.

Mothers Today
441 Lexington Avenue
New York, NY 10017
867-4820

A bimonthly magazine for expectant parents and parents of four-year-olds and under.

Parent's*
685 Third Avenue
New York, NY 10017
878-8700

A monthly magazine for expectant parents and parents of preteens and under.

Practical Parenting Newsletter
8326A Minnetonka Boulevard

Deephaven, MN 55391
612-475-1505

A bimonthly newsletter for expectant parents and parents of grade school age children and under.

Sesame Street Parents*
P.O. Box 52000
Boulder, CO 80322-2000

Provides information for parents about children age two through six, as well as a specially-sized little magazine for your children to read and color in, featuring favorite Sesame Street characters.

Twins Magazine
P.O. Box 12045
Overland Park, KS 66212
800-821-5533

The only bimonthly national magazine for parents of twins.

Working Mother
135 West 50th Street
New York, NY 10020
445-6100

A monthly magazine for parents of infants through teens.

about the authors

Kelly Ashton holds a B.A. from Yale University and an M.B.A. from Harvard University. She is the mother of three-year-old Alexander and writes and speaks on child-related topics.

Pamela Weinberg graduated from Brandeis University and is the mother of Rebecca, four, and Benjamin, one. She formerly ran Hospitality Dynamics, a food and lifestyle public relations firm.